# My JOURNEY To GRACE

# My JOURNEY To GRACE

*What I Learned
about Jesus in the Dark*

CINDY HYLES SCHAAP

XULON PRESS

Xulon Press
2301 Lucien Way #415
Maitland, FL 32751
407.339.4217
www.xulonpress.com

Edited by Linda Tucker
Cup and Quill Editing LLC

Paperback ISBN-13: 978-1-6322-1178-1

Ebook ISBN-13: 978-1-6322-1179-8

# Dedication

This book is dedicated to:

God - my Heavenly Father,
Jesus Christ the Son of God - my Savior and Friend,
The Holy Spirit of God- my Helper, Comforter and Guide.

Jesus,Trinity, Three in One
It is–always has been–and forever will be–only about You!

Thank you for leaving me your beautiful Word, and for letting me take
this faith journey with You!

I love you!
Cindy

# Table of Contents

A Special Acknowledgement

To my dear children:

Ken and Candace Schaap
Todd and Jaclynn Weber

We are a broken family, but a family fueled by the strength of the Lord and bubbling over with the joy of the Lord.

Humanly speaking, your faith and love have kept me going.

You are gifts from God, and I love you...

My Charge to you:

Romans 12:1, *"Be not overcome of evil, but overcome evil with good."*

To my grandchildren:

Lyndsay Weber          Kenny Schaap
Ray Weber              Chloe Schaap
Lexy Weber             Clarke Schaap
Jayke Weber            Claire Schaap

I hand to you a much messier legacy than I ever dreamed I would. But I hope and pray that it points you straight to the love of Jesus.

Grammy loves you...!!!

And Jesus loves you so much more!!!!!!!!!

# Acknowledgements

*O*nly God could orchestrate the people and events He used as instruments to bring back the music to my life. Through the following people, I understand better how important our daily words and deeds are, especially when we may not even realize their impact. I must add that these people may or may not know that they are being mentioned in this book. The fact that they are mentioned does not mean that they would agree with everything I have written in its pages. Still I want them to know in print how much they have touched the broken chords and in some way helped to reawaken the symphony of my life

First of all, I want to thank every pastor and pastor's wife whose church I have attended on a regular basis in the past 7 years. Thank you for taking me in. I needed you all more than you know.

Pastor Jon and Liz Cuozzo
South Point Church
Crown Point, Indiana

Pastor Scott and Jenny Gray
Liberty Baptist Church
Durham, North Carolina

Pastor Stephen and Marsha Davey
Colonial Baptist Church
Cary, North Carolina

Pastor Tim and Sharon Rabon
Beacon Baptist Church
Raleigh, North Carolina

I thank every guest speaker whose preaching I sat under during the past 7 years. God met with me so many times through you.

Thank you to the following folks who came to be what I needed at just the time I needed them:

Al and Valerie Morales
Sarah Smith
Annie Lutz
Karen Kurtz
Putt Smith
Nancy Shambley
Megan Scheibner
Donna Bos
Angela Bequette
Ed and Audrey Book
Etta Stadtmiller
Candace Davey
Carolann Capaci
Faye Jalbert
Tim and Carla Curington
Renee Cox
Joann Cox
Janet Moore
Bridget Trammell
Cathy Kimmel
Jeanine Nelson
John and Brenda Chandler
David and Kristy Heinbaugh

Thank you to the following people who offered financial support for 4-7 years:

Pastor Bruce and Tammy Goddard
John and Yulie Stancil
Linda Wittig
Jane Sunde

Thank you to the following Christian Counselors:

Sherry Allchin
Gwen Paul
Carol Williams

Thank you to everyone who sent a card, a note, a voicemail, or a message, Instagram or Facebook post on social media in those early days of heartbreak. I didn't answer most of them, but they all helped to carry me through some of the most difficult days of my life

Thank you to my sister Becky Smith for listening after Mom died–and to all of my family–I love you!

# Foreword

*A*s a little boy I remember many a morning, when coming down the stairs from my bedroom, I would see my mom sitting in a recliner reading from a well-worn Bible. Other times she would be on her knees in front of that same recliner spending time in prayer. It was quite a powerful example to me of consistency and dependence. She was consistent in her relationship with Jesus Christ, and this showed me and the rest of our family her faith and dependence on Him. Somehow knowing she loved Jesus gave me even more confidence in her love for me, as well as in her love for the rest of my family. But she wasn't the pious type. She was a fun mom, who played games, made great meals and made our home a happy and welcoming place.

Mom loved Jesus and her family in such a way that people began to ask her for advice. Soon she was a sought-after speaker and counselor. She wrote books on family and books on being a woman of faith. As a kid, I remember carrying boxes of books for her from our storage area and watching her carefully pack and ship to churches and bookstores all over America. We would often ship books that my father had authored too. He also was well-known; a Baptist preacher who travelled the country passionately sharing messages in hopes of inspiring people to love Jesus and serve Him with their lives. Eventually Dad became the pastor of one of America's largest churches and was even named one of America's 50 most influential Christians by a well-known Evangelical publication. My family helped people strengthen their families, learn the Bible, and know Jesus; and I was pretty proud of it.

Unfortunately, that all came crashing down. In 2012, my father was arrested for criminal behavior related to his dealings with a female member of the church youth department. The saga played out on national news for several days and in the Chicago news market for several months. Three decades of Christian ministry, two dozen books, and over a decade of leading a megachurch were all overshadowed by a terrible scandal. My father was sentenced to 12 years in a federal prison. The rest of our family was stunned to say the least. A new and completely unexpected turn in our lives had come, and we all felt quite alone and confused.

Throughout that terrible ordeal, my mom kept that well-worn Bible, close along with a daily routine of prayer and a pretty consistent schedule. However, the nice neat lines of her life that allowed her to write about faith and family were now a tangled and frayed mess. She was entering a new season where she could no longer speak to thousands, but instead would have to listen and suffer in silence. She was forced to make a thousand painful decisions, and she found herself away from the only church she'd ever known. Yet she continued to love the Lord and her family. Through some pretty dark days, she chose to avoid the blame game and instead to move on with her life. She started a new career, built her own life and found a depth in her faith that she had never known was there.

When you spend a lifetime talking to God and letting Him talk to you and continue to pursue Him through the ups and downs, He eventually gives you a special glimpse of how He does things. Let's call it a "behind the scenes tour." He does this for simple people who choose to depend on Him despite their failures and imperfections. The book you're holding is one such behind the scenes tour. It's not a tell-all written to set the record straight or to justify decisions that have been made. No, rather it's a private glimpse of how Jesus walks people through the darkness. It's a unique view of His mercies in the face of our failures. It's a reminder that when you walk through the valley with the shadow, He is with us and He won't let us go.

My Mom has proven to be a great student. She has learned much through this difficult journey. I pray that anyone who's ever had to walk in the dark will benefit from the lessons Jesus taught her in seasons of grief and confusion. Jesus is wonderful! I trust that as you read this, you'll come to agree with me.

Ken Schaap
Founding Pastor
FaithWay Church

# Preface

*I* walked into the Federal Building with my two children and their spouses by my side. We passed through the security checkpoint and entered the elevator that would take us upstairs to the room where my husband of 33 years would have much of his future determined. When we stepped off the elevator onto the second floor, I saw a lineup of people I had known and loved. They were there to show support. The courtroom was small, so most of them could not get in to watch the proceedings. Instead, they stood in the hallway and waited. I recall their sad, compassionate faces. My emotions were mixed.–I appreciated their support, but I also did not want anyone to be there. I didn't want to be there. I didn't want my children to be there. I was not *supposed* to be there.

I was thinking, "Hey everybody, I am a good little Sunday school girl; I am not supposed to be here. I don't belong in this world!" I felt some resentment about the behavior of those who had brought me into a world that I had carefully tried to avoid. I had made choices all of my life that should not have brought me to where I was on that day–March 20, 2013. I thought it was ironic that it was the first day of spring. I, Cindy Schaap, was not supposed to be there. *Why God? Why have You brought me here? And Who are You?*

When my children and I entered the actual courtroom, it was almost full. I informed one of the ladies in uniform that we were the family of the defendant, and we couldn't find a place to sit. Her reply–"The seats in the front are for the victim and the victim's family; you will have to sit along the back wall. "I recall wondering why my children and I were being treated as if we were supposed to be in the defendant's chair.

Even now, when I observe people arguing on social media about victims and their perpetrators, I wonder who is watching out for the spouses and children of the perpetrators.

As we settled into our seats, I felt the urge again to cry out, "I am a good little Sunday school girl; I am not supposed to be here!"

Instead, I spent almost every second of the rest of my moments in that courtroom silently chanting the lyrics to what had become my fight song:

**"I know Who goes before me**
**I know Who stands behind**
**The God of angel armies is always by my side**
**The One Who reigns forever; He is a Friend of mine.**
**The God of angel armies is always by my side!"**

The lyrics played on an endless loop. I was neither the defendant nor the victim. Still, I was in a fight not only for my sanity but also for my life. My fight song was among the weapons I used in my battle to survive.

The sentence was passed. My husband, Jack, had pleaded guilty in a plea bargain for 10 years. Instead, the judge gave him 12 years. Finally, the dreaded day we had anticipated for 21 months was finished. It was the first day of spring, ironically, The ordeal was over. All I wanted was to go home.

The children and I walked out of the courtroom to find the press in our faces. We made no comment to anyone; I had nothing I wanted to say. I didn't want to hurt anybody–not my husband and not the victim. In hindsight, if I had said anything at all to the throngs gathered, it would have been, "Hey everybody, I don't belong here. I am a good little Sunday school girl." And to God, I would have said, "I love You, and I trust You, but I don't know Who You are. Who are You?"

Seven years have passed since my now-ex-husband was sentenced, and I have not scratched the surface of all there is to know about God. However, I have learned that He wants to be known and that His greatness is inexhaustible. I have learned that it is Jesus who watches over betrayed spouses, children, and other unnamed victims. This awareness has left me genuinely perplexed, humbled, and even embarrassed by His kindness.

I am still learning wonderful things about both Jesus and myself.

Among the most impactful things I have learned is that I am not that good little Sunday school girl, after all. Perhaps I was no better than individuals who have sat in the defendant's chair and are now locked behind prison doors. This epiphany was the key that unlocked the door to my new life and made it possible for me to step forward. That may have been the lesson that I most needed to learn.

It turns out that I am not that good little Sunday school girl, and Jesus is all I could ever dream He would be and more.

# Chapter 1
## Finding Mercy in the Shadows

When I was born on November 30, 1959, my parents were pastoring a church with a congregation of hundreds. I suppose I lived a "staged" life from the very beginning. That is not to say my family and I were not genuine in our mission. Instead, we were always observed by many people.

I was asked to give my first speech to a large congregation when I was five years old. The church had bought new winter coats for my three siblings and me as a Christmas gift. My father called us up to the platform and asked each of us to say "thank you" into the microphone. As the youngest, my turn was last. I stood there and cried. My dad attempted to coax me into saying, "thank you," to no avail; I barely said a word.

I was not a child who did everything right. There is no such child, of course, but as the baby of my family, I was way down on the list of candidates. I was a daydreamer, a distracted child. I was comfortable being alone. I had a one-track mind, and I tended to be absentminded. ADHD was not talked about in those days, but I suspect I might have had a mild case. My behavior aside, I had tender feelings for God from a young age. I wanted to be Jesus' friend. Dozens of years passed before I understood that I was good enough.

Life was pretty normal until I was about eleven years old. In 1970, *Christian Life* magazine published an article that proclaimed my father's ministry to be the "World's Largest Sunday School." Around the same time, our church started an elementary school, a junior high school, high school, and then a college. As the child of two icons, I developed a serious "inferiority complex."

I have no regrets about how I was raised. I am so thankful for my parents. In our church, I walked amongst "salt of the earth," Midwestern

Christians who lived as if they genuinely loved Jesus. They also seemed to love me because I was the daughter of their pastor and wife. I loved and admired so many of them then, as I do now.

As the ministry expanded in its outreach, I met thousands of wonderful people from all over the United States and the world. I feel blessed to have had the opportunity to connect with and to learn from so many. This book is not intended as a judgment or a "put down" to any ministry or fellow Christian. Anyone who believes that Jesus is the Son of God and that He is their Savior, is my brother or sister in Christ. I am commanded to love them just as God the Father loves His only begotten Son.

*John 17:11, "And I am no more in the world, but these are in the world, and I come to thee. Holy Father, keep through thine own name those whom thou hast given me, **that may be one, as we are.**"*

Thus, this book is the medium I have chosen to describe my journey. As in any fleshly journey, I have carried conceptions and misconceptions. I do not blame anyone for my past misconceptions. For example, during my journey as a pastor's daughter, I imagined that I had to strive to please God to "win" His pleasure. I was taught "salvation by faith" from a young age, and I accepted that salvation. After a while, however, I lived my post-salvation life with a "works" mentality.

I was brought up with stringent rules. In the process of striving to keep those rules, I failed to grasp the mercy and grace of Jesus, Who had laid down His life for me. Again, I point a finger only at myself when I admit this.

There were seasons in my life when I strived so hard to please Jesus, to please my parents, to please my fellow parishioners, to please my friends around the country, and to please the world. (It is tiring just to write that.) I thought I was doing pretty well. In hindsight, that may be one of the greatest misconceptions I carried in my heart.

In other seasons, I found myself falling short. Many of my spiritual leaders emphasized personal character. I first realized that I could not measure up to such expectations during my very backward adolescent years, and I carried a sense of inferiority beyond my 50th birthday.

When one is trying to measure up to a Holy God, the result is guilt. The byproduct of such guilt is fear. I became a very fearful individual. For instance, if I forgot to read my Bible in the morning, I expected the day to go poorly. I saw having a bad day as God's punishment for not measuring up in my Bible reading, my punctuality, or in the shining of my shoes. I take responsibility for my thoughts. Since coming face to face with the mercy of Jesus, I am not afraid to take responsibility for such erroneous thinking.

When a person is trying to measure up to people, the result will often be a sense of shame. When trying to measure up to the expectations of thousands of people, the result is a public shame. These are feelings that I experienced from adolescence and for decades after that.

In 2012, public shame overtook reality for a time. All that I had built personally ground to a screeching halt when my husband of thirty-three years went to prison after pleading guilty to a crime, about which I had known nothing. Everything I had attempted until that point had seemingly failed. Satan tried to humiliate me, but I did not succumb. Why? Because Jesus and His Holy Spirit had already started the work of peeling away the shame of my thoughts, layer by layer.

Something went wrong with my marriage. Had I known what it was, I would have gotten help. The last thing I wanted to do was to live out a hypocritical marriage before so many people that I genuinely loved.

I lived in the shadow of a looming storm. I couldn't pinpoint what exactly was happening, and looking back, I am sure that I was in denial. Part of that denial came from God's protection over my life. The other part came from my effort to walk in my faith; I believed that if I prayed and tried hard enough, God would always come through in the ways that I had manipulated. That is, I trusted so much of my life's outcome to my character. I loved Jesus, and I held to the ideal that if I strived to please Him, then eventually He would make it all better. The problem was that I defined "better" as outcomes that aligned with my desires.

## God Is Not Mad At Me.

> *Isaiah 54:9,10 "For this is as the waters of Noah unto me: for as I have sworn that the waters of Noah should no more go over the earth; so have I sworn that I would not be wroth with thee, nor rebuke thee.*
>
> *For the mountains shall depart, and the hills be removed; but My kindness shall not depart from thee, neither shall the **covenant of my peace** be removed, saith the Lord that hath mercy on thee."*

In his book "The Gospel of Peace," Dr. James B. Richards writes, "If someone came on the scene and proclaimed that God was going to judge the world by water, we all would quickly realize the error." [1]God tells us that He will never again destroy the world with a flood. In the same verse, he also declares that He will never again be mad at me.

When this verse became clear to me, I was dumbfounded. I was a fifty-something lady who had been saved since the age of five. I had heard about Calvary since childhood; I should have understood that the heart of such a marvelous Savior would be merciful. But I didn't. I was not only surprised; I was dumbfounded, and I was excited.

I had the ear of many women in those days. I was the pastor's wife of a megachurch and spoke to thousands of ladies yearly. I wanted to share what I was learning, so I began to try. I was leery of revealing all I was learning; in my mind, that would be too risky. I was afraid I might be misunderstood. I was scared that people might mistake my view of God's unlimited mercy as an attack on personal holiness. I believe in personal holiness, but I do not believe in public humiliation. I also believe that all personal rules must be held up against the light of God's

---

[1] Dr. James B. Richards, *The Gospel of Peace,* (Orrstown, PA, MileStones International Publishers, 2002)

inerrant Word to ensure that tradition and opinions are not exalted above the Lord.

## Jesus Will Never Be Mad At Me.

I shared what I felt safe sharing, but in my heart, the view I held about God would never be the same. I wanted to shout God's mercy from the housetops, and I still want to do this. The public failure and all of the loss that became a part of my life as of July 2012 could have destroyed me. The Cindy Schaap of a few years earlier would have been ashamed and afraid of what she had done wrong to deserve such punishment from an angry God. Fortunately, the Cindy Schaap, who had her world rocked in 2012, had begun to grasp the Gospel of Peace–the Good News.

> *Luke 2:10-11,13,14, "And the angel said unto them, Fear not: for, behold, I bring you **good tidings of great joy**, which shall be to all people. For unto you is born this day in the city of David, a Saviour, which is Christ the Lord. And suddenly there was with the angel a multitude of the heavenly host praising God and saying, Glory to God in the highest, and on earth **peace, goodwill toward men**."*

I used to read verse 14 and wonder why there was no "goodwill" **among** men. Hatred and violence seem to be more typical of the behavior on earth between people. But the "goodwill" in Luke chapter 2 is not talking about the goodwill **among** the people on earth; it is talking about the goodwill **toward** men from our Heavenly Father.

When Jesus cried, "It is finished," on the Cross, He made a way for me to appease his anger forever. It was not my own "good little Sunday school girl" ways that appeased his anger. On the contrary, mine, above all others, would fall way too short.

All I had to do was say "yes" to salvation and accept the gifts of the mercy and grace of God the Father through Jesus Christ His Son. Wahoo! I AM GOOD WITH GOD; JESUS AND I ARE PERMANENTLY AT PEACE. And so are you if you have accepted Him. I would not impose any human tradition upon you that would steal from you such freedom and "great joy." There is no man-made rule to which you are to be held accountable for righteousness, and there is no Biblical sin that God cannot and will not forgive.

Dr. Richards says, "The covenant with Noah was sealed with a rainbow. The covenant of peace was sealed in the blood of Jesus."[2]

When I see a rainbow on a "Gay" flag, I see a symbol of the mercy of the Jesus Who loves me and every sinner (We all have sinned.) with unconditional love and mercy, and Who stands ready to forgive and redeem those Who turn to Him to be their Savior.

Before July 2012, I had no idea how dark my personal world would become. I did not yet understand how brilliantly Jesus would shine in contrast to my very dark world. But I had begun to see the shadows of a storm coming. In those shadows, I saw how bright Jesus' righteousness is compared to my own "good deeds." Looking back, I see that Jesus prepared me for what He knew was lying ahead on my horizon. His preparation in my life shows what a holy and harmless God He is.

I got my first glimpse of Jesus in the dark during the shadowy lull before my storm, although I did not see anger or judgment. Rather, in my first glimpse of Jesus in my darkness, I saw the stark brilliance of His mercy. Just one glimpse of Jesus in my darkness, and I sensed that nothing would ever be the same.

---

[2] Dr. James B. Richards, *The Gospel of Peace*, (Orrstown, PA, Miles Stones International Publishers, 2002)

*Finding Mercy In The Shadows*

# GLOSSARY OF SCRIPTURE

*UNITY -*

*John 13:34,35, "A new commandment I give unto you, That ye **love one another**; as I have loved you, that ye also **love one another**. By this shall all men know that ye are my disciples, if ye **have love one to another**."*

*John 15:12, "This is my commandment, That ye **love one another**, as I have loved you."*

*John 15;17, "These things I command you**, that ye love one another**."*

*John 17:1, "And now I am no more in the world, but these are in the world, and I come to thee. Holy Father, keep through thine own name those whom thou hast given me, **that they may be one, as we are**."*

*John 17:21-23, "**That they all may be one**; as thou, Father, art in me, and I in thee, **that they also may be one in us**: that the world may believe that thou hast sent me. And the glory which thou gavest me I have given them; **that they may be one, even as we are one**: I in them, and thou in me, **that they may be made perfect in one**; and that the world may know that thou hast sent me, and hast loved them as thou hast loved me."*

*I Corinthians 12:12,13, "For as the body is one, and hath many members, and all the members of that one body, being many are one body: so also is Christ. **For by one Spirit are we all baptized into one body**, whether we be bond or free; and have all been made to drink into one Spirit."*

*I Corinthians 12:25, "That there should be no schism in the body; but that the members should **have the same care one for another.**"*

*I Peter 4:8, **"And above all things have fervent charity among your-selves:** for charity shall cover the multitude of sins."*

*I John 3:14, "We know that we have passed from death unto life, because **we love the brethren.** He that loveth not his brother abideth in death."*

*I John 3:23, "And this is his commandment, That we should believe on the name of his Son Jesus Christ, and **love one another,** as he gave us commandment."*

*GOSPEL OF PEACE -*

*Romans 10:3,4, "For they being ignorant of God's righteousness, and going about to establish their own righteousness, have not submitted themselves unto the righteousness of God."*

*Romans 10:15, "And how shall they preach, except they be sent? as it is written, How beautiful are the feet of them that preach the **gospel of peace,** and bring glad tidings of good things."*

*Romans 14:10, "But why dost thou judge thy brother? Or why dost thou set at nought thy brother? For we shall all stand before the judgment seat of Christ."*

# Chapter 2
Finding Love Before The Earthquake

*I* was in Bar Harbor, Maine, in the middle of a two-week retreat, when my then-husband came into our resort room and told me that he had been fired as pastor of the megachurch I had attended since I was a few weeks old. My father had been the pastor of the church for the first forty-one years of my life, and Jack became the pastor one month after my dad's death in 2001. This left me with virtually no time to grieve the loss of my father.

Jack was the pastor for eleven years. For several years, it seemed that everything he touched turned to gold, ministry wise. Looking back, however, I do not think I ever knew what hit me when we took over the ministry. First, my father, to whom I had been close, died. One month later, I "lost" my husband, who had never pastored before, to the extremely rigorous schedule of an inherited megachurch. Then, in 2002, my daughter got married and left our home. In 2003, my mother, still stricken with grief and loss after my father's passing, moved a thousand miles away to her hometown of Dallas, Texas. Finally, my son, Ken, the only child left at home, was already in a serious relationship with his future wife, Candace.

Nonetheless, I jumped in and got involved in several ministries of the church while also trying to keep our family together. There were many joyous times during those years, as we watched both of our children marry and start their families. Six of our eight grandchildren were born during those years.

Still, it was a lonely time for me. In hindsight, I was living in a state of great grief from the losses I had experienced. I believe that I may well have been grieving the significant loss that was yet to come. In other words, even then, indeed, especially then, Jesus and His Holy Spirit, were preparing me for the future.

Jesus' preparation started, as I remember, while I was reading a book entitled *A Love Worth Giving*, by Max Lucado.

I John 4:19, *"We love him because he first loved us."*

Even though I had wanted to be Jesus' friend, and I had possessed a tender heart for Him from childhood, I also held an unhealthy fear of Him.

> I John 4:18, *"There is no fear in love, but perfect love casteth out fear: because fear hath torment. He that feareth is not made perfect in love."*

Somewhere in my reading, I became aware that our love for God is to be a response to Jesus' unconditional love for us. The song "Jesus Loves Me" was one I had sung as a child, and I taught it to my children and grandchildren as well. My head knew that Jesus loved me, but my heart felt His love and acceptance were conditional. I thought I had to earn both daily, if not moment by moment.

## Perceiving God's Love

> I John 3:16 says, *"Hereby perceive we the love of God because he laid down his life for us..."*

The Greek word *"perceive"* or *"ginosko,"* in this verse means to "come to know; to understand." I knew the love of God, but I had little understanding of it until a few years before the "earthquake" of heartbreak arrived.

Webster's dictionary defines "perceive" as to understand with the senses. Since there are five senses, I started a lifelong search for God's love by searching it through those senses. I bought a journal and started a practice that is still a part of my daily ritual. Each morning, after I read my Bible, I write down everything good that happened to me the day before. I made a rule that I would never write anything negative in these journals. I take a few seconds each morning to read over what I have written, and to thank Jesus for each good thing that took place "yesterday."

At least twice a day, I ask God to show Himself to me. I pray that He will open my eyes and help me look for and see Him. I also ask His Holy Spirit to speak to me. I ask Him to open my ears to listen for and hear Him. I also ask the Holy Spirit to lead me and help me to understand (perceive) Him and His leadership. These rituals are part of my morning routine and also part of my bedtime ritual. Interestingly, many of my encounters with God's love have taken place while I was alone in the middle of the night.

This is a simple practice, but it has changed me. I see this practice, and more importantly, the way Jesus shows His unconditional love for me, as the main event that both prepared me for, and carried me through, my darkness.

Jesus loves to be found. He loves to show His love to His children. It amazes me how personally He reveals Himself. I have prayed some really strange prayers–prayers that wouldn't mean a thing to anyone but me–and God has answered them so sweetly.

So, what are the five senses? They are:

Sight
Sound
Touch
Smell
and last but not least–Taste.

On any given day, I may be grinning and praising God under my breath for His love during the mundane moments of life.

*I see a rainbow and say, "I see your love, Jesus; I know You love me, and I love You." Rainbows are just one of the many symbols that have become a "thing" between my Friend Jesus and me.

*I hear a song in the night–just the right song at just the right time, and I say, "I hear your love Jesus; I know you love me, and I love you too."

*I touch the cheek of my youngest grandchild, and I say to my Friend, "I feel your love, Jesus; I know You love me, and I love You too."

*I put my nose way too far into the bag of Starbucks coffee and say, "I smell Your love Jesus; I know You love me, and I love You too."

*I taste the warmth of a Starbucks coffee or any food for that matter, and I say, "I taste Your love Jesus; I know You love me, and I love You too."

There are so many stories that I could share; to me, they are nothing short of miraculous. They are stories of the big and seemingly unimportant ways that God shows Himself to me. An entire book could be written about them, but for now, let me say that God is no respecter of persons; He does not discriminate. He loves all of His children the same, just as I love all of my children and grandchildren the same–only He is a much better parent. He wants you to seek Him, and He wants to show Himself to you. He loves to make His love personal, and He loves to make it clear.

Jeremiah 29:12-14a, *"Then shall ye call upon me, and ye shall go and pray unto me, and I will hearken unto you. And ye shall seek me and find me when ye shall search for me with all your heart. And I will be found of you, saith, the Lord..."*

I love the song entitled *"Good, Good Father."* The words to the familiar contemporary song say:

*"I've heard a thousand stories of what they think you're like, But I've heard the tender whisper of love in the dead of night. And you tell me that you're pleased and that I'm never alone."*

And the chorus says:

> *"You're a good, good Father*
> *That's Who You are, Who You are,*
> *And I'm loved by You.*
> *That's Who I am, Who I am."*

That is precisely who I am—Just a messy sinner who is loved by my good, good Heavenly Father.

## Rooted And Grounded In His Love

Ephesians 3:17 puts it this way, *"That Christ may dwell in your heart by faith; that ye being rooted and grounded (or established or founded) in love."*

My identity is in the love of Jesus, and it was rooted in that love on that fateful day of July 30, 2012. I am so thankful that God and His Holy Spirit had been teaching me about that love in preparation for the trial that was coming up ahead. If my identity had been in anything else, I am almost sure that I could not have survived.

> Ephesians 3:18,19, *"May be able to comprehend with all saints what is the breadth, and length, and depth, and height, And to know the love of Christ which passeth knowledge, that ye might be filled with all the fulness of God."*

It is impossible for mere flesh to fully comprehend, perceive, or understand the love of God. Imagine how high God's love must be. It is high enough that I have seen the most beautiful rainbow when riding a jet over 10,000 feet in the air—but it is much higher than that.

Imagine how long the love of Jesus must be. It is long enough to be patient through the multitude of all of my sins and failures–but it is much longer than that.

Imagine how broad the love of Jesus must be. It is broad enough to carry the burdens that threaten to break my spirit–but it is much broader than that.

Imagine how deep the love of God must be. It is deeper than the deepest part of the ocean, but it is much deeper than that.

Jesus wants to take a lifelong hike with us. On this hike, He wants to be the Teacher, and He wants us to be the students. He wants to educate us continually on all of the facets of His love. On that hike through life, He wants to show us so many wonders; some are stunning to the entire world, and some are personal and just for you. He is probably showing Himself and His wonders to you right now. Indeed, He probably has been all day long. It is just that so few of us look for Him. We get so entangled with the "cares of this world, and the deceitfulness of riches" (Matthew 13:22) that we get offended by God. Then we stumble "and become unfruitful," rather than noticing that He is right beside us, loving us, showing Himself to us, and speaking His love to us.

To notice His love and to perceive or comprehend this love is to be "filled with all the fulness of God." It brings the fulness of the Holy Spirit into our lives. That fulness manifests itself in the "fruit of the Spirit:"

> Galatians 5:22,23, "*And the fruit of the Spirit is love, joy, peace, longsuffering, gentleness, goodness, faith, meekness, temperance: against such, there is no law.*"

## Love And The Romans Road

My father used the Romans Road as a method for presenting the Gospel. The Romans Road is a map of verses found in the book of Romans that summarizes how to be saved and inherit eternal life. I am not sure where the Romans Road originated, but my father received some credit for making it better known, I am so pleased that God used my father in that way. Please allow me to share my "Cindy" version of the Romans Road.

1. We Are All A Mess.

> Romans 3:10, *"There is none righteous, no not one."*

> Romans 3:23, *"For all have sinned,* and come short of the glory of God."

2. We Have A Great, Big Wonderful God.

> Genesis 1:1, *"In the beginning, God created the Heaven and the earth."*

> Psalms 121:2, *"My help comes from the Lord, which made heaven and earth."*

3. God's Only Name Is Jesus.

> Acts 4:12, *"Neither is there salvation in any other: for there is none other name under heaven, given among men, whereby we must be saved."*

> Philippians 2:10,11, *"That at the name of Jesus every knee should bow, of things in Heaven, and things in earth and things under the earth. And that every tongue should confess that Jesus Christ is Lord, to the glory of God the Father."*

4. Jesus Loves You With Unconditional Love.

Romans 5:8, *"But God commendeth (proves, demonstrates, displays) his love toward us, in that, while we were yet sinners, Christ died for us."*

Jesus died on the cross to pay the penalty and bear the shame of our messy sin. He rose from the dead to conquer death.

5. Jesus Wants To Be Your Savior And Friend And To Share His Love With You Forever In This Life And In Heaven. He Wants You To Receive His Love By Calling On His Name And Professing Him As Your Lord And Savior. This Simple Act Of Faith Will Make You His Child Today And From Now On.

Romans 10:13, *"For whosoever shall call on the name of the Lord shall be saved."*

And I would add, as I recently did to my atheist friend, "If you don't believe this, just ask God to show Himself to you. If you mean it, I promise you He will.

## A Vision From God

Isaiah 30:14, *"And he shall break it as the breaking of the potters' vessel that is broken in pieces; he shall not spare: so that there shall not be found in the bursting of it a sherd to take fire from the hearth, or to take water withal out of the pit."*

On the morning of July 31, 2012, I realized that my life was changed forever. I believe I saw a vision from the Lord that morning, and I have relived that vision many times.

I was sitting in the middle of the rubble of a great earthquake, and there was nothing left. It was just me and the rubble. I stood up and walked away. I did not know yet what the consequences of Jack's actions would be or how the future would unfold. Still, I was already sure that nothing about my life would be the same—nothing except my identity.

I would no longer be a pastor's wife.
I would no longer be a wife.
I would no longer attend the church I had attended my entire life.
I would no longer live in the area where I had lived my whole life.
I would no longer live in the house I loved, where I had lived for thirty years.
I would no longer work the job or serve in the ministry where I had served in one capacity or another since high school.

But I knew who I was; I was who I had always been. I was a person unconditionally loved by God. In my vision, when I looked at the rubble of the earthquake around me, and I stood up to walk away from it all, Someone was holding my hand. He didn't look angry. He seemed pleased; He looked like He loved me. His love shone brighter than the sun on that July morning. It has shined brightly every night and every day since then. It is shining brightly right now where I am and also where you are. We just have to look for Him.

The sun shown so brightly on July 31, 2012, yet it was one of the darkest days of my life. Even in the darkness, I could see so clearly that God is love, and love is what Jesus looks like in the dark.

*Finding Love*

# A GLOSSARY OF SCRIPTURE

John 14:21, *"He that hath my commandments, and keepeth them, He it is that loveth me, and he that loveth me shall be loved of my Father, and **I will love him** and will manifest myself to him."*

John 16:27, ***"For the Father himself loveth you,*** *because have loved me, and have believed that I came out from God."*

Acts 28:26,27, *"Saying, Go unto this people, and say, Hearing ye shall hear, and shall not understand, and seeing ye shall see, and not perceive. For the heart of this people is waxed gross, and their ears are dull of hearing, and their eyes have they closed, lest they should see with their eyes, and hear with their ears, and understand with their heart, and should be converted, and I should heal them."*

I John 3:16, ***"Hereby perceive we the love of God,*** *because he laid down his life for us: and we ought to lay down our lives for the brethren."*

I John 4:7-12, "Beloved, let us love one another: for love is of God; and everyone that loveth is born of God, and knoweth God. *He that loveth not knoweth God; for **God is love.**"*

***In this was manifested the love of God towards us,*** *because that God sent his only begotten Son into the world, that we might live through him Herein is love, not that we loved God, but **that he loved us,** and sent his Son to be the propitiation for our sins. Beloved, if **God so loved us,** we ought* *also to love one another. No man hath seen God at any time. If we love one another, 'God dwelleth in us, and **his love is perfected in us**"*

*I John 4:16,17a, And we have known and believed the love that God hath to us. **God is love;** and he that dwelleth in love dwelleth in God and God in him. Herein is our love made perfect...*

# Chapter 3
## A Matter of the Heart

On the morning of Tuesday, July 31st, 2012, I flew home by myself from Bar Harbor, Maine, to Chicago, Illinois. I had a layover in Boston. Jack and I had driven to Maine, intending to take a two-and-a-half-week vacation. I had not packed carefully, so I had quite a bit of luggage to drag through the Boston airport. My traveling experience was my first lesson about living life on my own.

My son in law picked me up at the Chicago Midway airport and took me home where I saw my children for the first time since they had heard the news. We were all in shock and very confused. Jack drove home and arrived the next day, August 1st.

From August 1st until September 18th, we waited to see what Jack's future would hold. During that time, we were watched by the FBI, and we experienced an FBI raid. It wasn't unusual to see a large, black SUV trailing us. I recall crying a lot and feeling agitated because Jack had brought me into this world. I was also afraid and concerned about Jack. I tried to encourage him, but I also kept my mouth shut. I could not say a lot of what I was thinking; I didn't know what to think.

I came home from a simple trip to the grocery store on Tuesday, September 18th, and found my husband waiting at the garage door for me. It was around 2:00 p.m.

He greeted me with, "I am going to jail tomorrow." Jack was considered a flight risk, so he would be detained until his sentence was passed on January 15th of the following year. That Tuesday evening was the last night that I would ever spend in my home of thirty years with my husband of thirty-three years.

Our four children met us at the house the following morning to drive to the courthouse. Our daughter and son in law lived directly across the street from us. A babysitter was going to watch all of our grandchildren while we were gone. Jack walked across the street to say goodbye to all of them. He went over twice. The first time I stayed behind. I have always hated goodbyes, and I didn't feel I could bear to watch. The second time I went with him and watched him say goodbye.

At about 10:00 a.m. on Wednesday, September 19th, 2012, we arrived at the courthouse. I walked past the press by Jack's side, followed by our four children. We entered the building, walked through security, and I hugged Jack. Then, he walked away, and that was the last time I saw him as a free man.

The next time I saw him was at his hearing one week later. A few days after he left for jail, I was called to the attorney's office to pick up a plastic bin with the clothes that he had worn to jail–a sports jacket, dress shirt and tie, and his Stacy Adams shoes. This time, he shuffled in with his wrists and ankles chained and dressed in jail garb. It was one of the saddest sights I have seen, or ever will see. A heart-wrenching experience. The only way I made it through the experience was by God's amazing grace. I think I was also in a bit of shock and, therefore, numb.

On September 19th, 2012, I went to bed living alone for the first time in 33 years. I am thankful for social media and the outpouring of Facebook posts and letters that I received during that time. Though I answered very few of the letters, I appreciate every one of them; they were my lifeline.

I spent my first year alone, laying low and waiting. My daughter and I visited Jack at his detainment in Valparaiso, Indiana, once a week. I was only allowed to speak to Jack on a TV screen for several months. It was in June of the next year that I first saw him in person at a jail in downtown Chicago.

I began to get frightened at night. For a while, I slept on my daughter and son-in-law's couch. Eventually, my son in law built me a small bedroom in their basement, where I stayed from sundown until sunup each day. The room was a surprise. Todd made it while I was on a trip to Florida. It was a lovely surprise and such a kind gesture. My memory of that room is one I will always hold dear.

## Looking At My Heart

My most vivid memory of the first year of Jack's incarceration involved the seven months of counseling I received. I am a fan of Christian counseling, and The Biblical Counseling Center provided seven months of ministry to my soul. I left feeling cleansed and refreshed after each weekly meeting.

At some point during those seven months, I told a counselor my"whole story" beginning in childhood. I will not share with you all that transpired during those meetings, but I took a long look at my heart that year. I have not been completely the same since then.

If you had asked me before those seven months if my heart were right with the Lord, I would have probably answered, "Yes." I loved Jesus, and I read my Bible and prayed daily. I had already begun a fascinating journey of exploring His unconditional love and mercy.

I was also a public speaker and hosted women's conferences. I traveled to several states each year to talk about Jesus, and I was often described as"real" and"transparent" in my speaking.

However, while living my public life, and despite working hard to follow all the rules I had been taught, I lost touch with matters of the heart. Being a good Christian had become a garment I put on and a duty that I performed.

Though I talked with God, and I was honest with God, I didn't think much about what God saw when He looked at my heart. I shared my heart with God regularly. In hindsight, though, I don't think I shared all of my heart with Him. Prayer had become a tool that I manipulated to get what I wanted. I felt that if I did what I was supposed to do, then God was obligated to give me what I asked for based on His promises. Of course, I always fell short—we all do. As a result, I suffered from both an inferiority and a superiority complex.

I placed more emphasis on others' adherence to my standards than I did to my heart attitude towards those people. I recall feeling angry if I saw a woman who was not dressed the way that I thought she should be dressed in my presence. Even if a woman was not biblically immodest, if she were not dressed the way I thought she should be, I felt furious.

In the dark days of that first year on my own, a kind counselor helped me to take a good look at my heart. I didn't just glance at it; I looked at what was inside. I held both my good deeds and the fury I found in my heart up to the light and compared them to the heart of Jesus. I was embarrassed by what I found.

I loved people. However, when I looked at my heart, I realized my self-righteousness got in the way of treating others tenderly and lovingly.

## Seeing Jesus' Heart

When my world seemed as dark as it could be, I saw the heart of Jesus clearly, and I was taken aback by what I saw.

One night, I awoke at 3:00 a.m., overcome with grief. I fell on my knees and prayed. That was when God allowed me to see His heart. I had nothing to offer God at that moment except raw grief and a boat-load of loss and failure. I am sure that I heard the Holy Spirit say to me that night, "I am pleased with you." That was when I saw the heart of God in the dark.

What is the heart of God like in the darkest valley?

1. The heart of God is tender.

2. The heart of God is easy to please.

3. The heart of God walks in when everyone and everything walks out.

I had been a good little Sunday school girl. I had loved God and wanted to be His friend. I loved people to the best of my ability, but my heart was not at all like Jesus' heart. And I was embarrassed.

I wanted to apologize to every person who my un-Christ-like heart may have affected. I have apologized to some of them.

In 2012, I found myself falling in love with broken people. I love everything that has to do with broken people. Why? Because I am one of them, and that is where I found Jesus' heart. It is with those who are broken.

As Christians, we have to be careful that we don't love only the broken people who are new Christians. We also must love those broken people who grew up in Sunday school, but who do not seem to get it right, according to others' expectations. That was always who I viewed myself to be. But Jesus is pleased with me. I know now that He only wants my heart.

In Luke 16:15, Jesus addresses the Pharisees, who are the only people who Jesus called out publicly, repeatedly, during His earthly ministry.

*"And he said unto them. Ye are they which justify yourselves before men, but God knoweth your hearts."*

I am not condemning any movement, church, or individual. I am trying to show you Who Jesus was to me in the dark.

Since 2012, I am more raw than I was previously in my conversations with God and His Holy Spirit. Sometimes, I tell Him something, and He puts the light on my heart. Then I realize that I am not being honest with Him and tell Him the whole truth.

Sometimes, I giggle at my attempt at Pharisaism."Oops, Jesus, you know that is not exactly true." Then I tell Him my heart, and He is pleased.

## Love God With All Your Heart

In all of our Pharisaical ways, we Christians fail to keep the biggest commandment of all.

The Jews are trying to keep over six hundred commandments, and I can't even keep one.

Mark 12:29,30, *"And Jesus answered him, the first of all commandments is, Hear O Israel; the Lord our God is one Lord:*

*And thou shalt love the Lord thy God with all thy heart, and with all thy soul, and with all thy mind, and with all thy strength: this is the first commandment."*

Jesus wants our hearts. This seems like a self-serving commandment, and of course, our Creator and Savior has every right to be self-serving. In the dark, I didn't see a self-serving Jesus. At Calvary, we certainly don't see a self-serving Jesus.

Jeremiah 32:41, *"Yea, I will rejoice over them to do them good, and I will plant them in this land assuredly, with my whole heart and with my whole soul."*

Jesus loves you and me and does us good with His whole heart. Wow! Just think how much heart that is! A whole lot of heart goes beyond all of the good that Jesus does for us. In return, Jesus asks us to try to put as much heart into our love and service for Him, as He faithfully does for us.

## Love Your Neighbor

And the second commandment is a spin-off from the first.

Mark 12:31, *"And the second is like, namely this, Thou shalt love thy neighbor as thyself. There is none other commandment greater than these"*

It sounds to me that a heart love for God leads, or ought to lead, to a heart love for people. God commands us to make loving people our highest priority other than loving God Himself.

One Mother's day, when my children were small, they brought me breakfast in bed. Jack was out of town, so they planned the menu on their own. My Mother's Day breakfast included cheese, saltine crackers, nacho cheese potato chips, and a chocolate chip cookie. I was not a junk food lover, even then, but I ate every bite. In my memory, that meal was among the most delightful I have ever eaten. That morning I penned these simple words to Jesus:

> *"Meekly and humbly, I give my life,*
> *Like a child who has nothing more to bring.*
> *Sweetly and kindly You accept my gift,*
> *Like a mother who wants no better thing.*
> *My life is one small thing.*
> *It's all I have to bring.*
> *But You'll take my small thing.*
> *For all You wanted is my heart."*

All Jesus wants is my heart. I gave it to Him more fully when we were alone in the dark. In return, Jesus showed me His heart. I saw a heart that was pleased with mine. His was such a lovely heart, and I could see it more clearly in the dark. I yearned for more of Jesus' heart to blend with my own.

Yes, there is a right and wrong that we see in the light of God's Word. And yes, there are consequences of sin. But at the center of it all is the loving, tender, unchangeable heart of a God who cares for people, including those who are broken people, more than anything else.

At the end of the day, the Christian life is simply a matter of the heart.

*A Matter Of The Heart*

# Glossary Of Scripture

*Deuteronomy 8:2, "And thou shalt remember all the way which the Lord thy God led thee these forty years in the wilderness, to humble thee, and to prove thee, to know what was in thine **heart**, whether thou wouldest keep his commandments, or no"*

*I Chronicles 28:9, "And thou, Solomon my son, know thou the God of thy father, and serve him with a perfect **heart** and with a willing mind: for the Lord searcheth all **hearts**, and understandeth all the imaginations of the thoughts: if thou seek him, he will be found of thee; but if thou forsake him, he will cast thee off for ever."*

*Psalms 26:2, "Examine me, O Lord, and prove me; try my reins and my **heart.**"*

*Psalms 78:37, "For their **heart** was not right with him, neither were they stedfast in his covenant."*

*Isaiah 29:13, "Wherefore the Lord said, Forasmuch as this people draw near me with their mouth, and with their lips do honor me but have **removed their heart far from me**, and **their fear toward me is taught by the precept of men.**"*

*Proverbs 3:5, "Trust in the Lord with all thine **heart**, and lean not unto thine own understanding."*

*Proverbs 4:23, "Keep thine **heart** with all diligence; for out of it are the issues of life."*

*Proverbs 14:30, "A sound **heart** is the life of the flesh: but envy the rottenness of the bones."*

*Proverbs 17:3, "The fining pot is for silver, and the furnace for gold: but the Lord trieth the **hearts.**"*

*Proverbs 21:2, "Every way of a man is right in his own eyes: but the Lord pondereth the **hearts.**"*

*Proverbs 23:7, "For as he thinketh in his **heart**, so is he"*

*Proverbs 23:26, "My son, give me thine **heart**, and let thine eyes observe my ways."*

*Matthew 15:8, "This people draweth nigh unto me with their mouth and honoureth me with their lips, but their **heart** is far from me."*

*Ephesians 6:6, "Not with eye service as men-pleasers, but as the servants of Christ, doing the will of God from the **heart.**"*

*Hebrews 3:10, "Wherefore I was grieved with that generation, and said, They do always err in their **heart**, and they have not known my ways."*

# Chapter 4
## Hearing The Voice Of God

*O*n September 19, 2012, Jack went to jail, and I started my life without him. His sentencing was supposed to take place on January 15, 2013, but it was delayed until March 20, 2013. The prosecution sought to give him three life sentences. Jack's attorney advised him to take a guilty plea and accept ten years in prison. The judge had the authority to make that sentence more lenient. Instead, he sentenced Jack to twelve years.

The kids and I prayed about what our future would look like. I was burdened by having to decide about my marriage on my own. The decision seemed too monumental to make by myself. When do you give up on a thirty-year marriage? When do you give up on the father of your children? Is it okay to give up at all?

## The Still, Small Voice

I was standing before my bathroom mirror in St. John, Indiana, when a still, small voice spoke one sentence of information to me. I would later come to believe that the voice was that of the Holy Spirit. That voice became my Friend during my first seven years alone.

Jack was still in detainment in a holding center in downtown Chicago. I visited him once a week. I rarely visited him alone, but one week I happened to go by myself. A dear friend drove me to the center and dropped me off. I went through security and then joined the group of loved ones who took the elevator together, escorted by a guard, twenty-some floors up to the visitors' room. We gathered in a holding place, and the bars shut behind us. That was an experience with which I never became comfortable.

I do not wish to share the details of this visit. This book is not about Jack or me or the horrific experiences that became a part of my life. Instead, it is about Jesus and Who He showed Himself to be during those experiences. Suffice it to say that on that night, it became apparent to me that our marriage was beginning to end.

I would not make a final decision about our marriage until almost a year later. I took my time because I valued the marriage covenant, and I valued what our family had been for many years. But on that June night, when the clock said 8:15, and the guard informed us that visiting hours were over, I hugged my husband. I quietly went down the elevator, thankfully, to the other side of those bars. I knew in my heart that I would not visit again, and I have not seen Jack since.

I am sharing these details because I want you to know that God Himself told me something in an ordinary place where I could not possibly have known or discovered the information on my own. He didn't speak out loud, and I had not asked Him for any information. Just "out of the blue," a sentence passed through my mind, and I knew I had to ask about it. When I did, I realized that I had been given a truth from the Lord that I needed to know.

I have never investigated the information I received, which has helped to preserve my sanity since my husband left. In hindsight, I believe that was a great decision on my part. Don't get me wrong—I have made many mistakes in these last years.

I once read that it is prideful to think one can handle any trial perfectly. I started my trial believing just that. I was soon made aware that I could not handle it perfectly.

I have not tried to discover any truth or wrongdoing, nor have I tried to right those wrongs done against me. I have asked God to show me what I needed to know so that I could decide what I needed to resolve. His Holy Spirit has been faithful to speak to me.

Until then, I had believed that God only spoke to women through a husband or a pastor. Though I loved my unique role as a woman and still do, in those days, I don't think my view of women was completely biblical. I do realize that the Bible defines a particular role for a husband and wife in marriage. However, in recent years, I have been influenced by some marriages I have observed, where the husband and wife share more of a partner role. I believe this enhances and also protects the oneness of marriage.

I have become stronger as an individual, because I have *had* to do so. That has changed my view about the love and respect that Jesus had for women in the New Testament. It has also changed my view of the respect that a husband and wife should share mutually for one another.

My trial left me without a husband or a pastor. If Jesus had not been faithful, I am convinced that I would not have survived the journey, the heartbreak, and the decisions that I faced. But Jesus was and is indeed faithful.

## Moving Forward

After much prayer, my son-in-law, Todd, took a position at a church in Durham, North Carolina. I decided that I would leave Indiana, or stay, depending on what my children did. After much soul searching and church hopping, I made the South Point Church of Crown Point, Indiana, my temporary church while we prayed, and I waited to see where God would have me go. I am thankful for my days under the pastorate of Jon Cuozzo and his wife, Liz. Eventually, I said my goodbyes to the South Point church family and moved South.

I was thrilled at the prospect of moving to the South and starting a new life. My parents had been raised in the South, and they loved it. My life had been on hold since Jack left, and I had basically been in hiding. I felt so ready to begin to live again.

I sold my house, packed the moving truck, and bought a townhouse in Durham, with the help of many amazing friends. I am so grateful to them, and yet most of the move seems like a blur now. I said a public goodbye to South Point Church, and I wrote a goodbye letter to the

First Baptist Church of Hammond and asked the new pastor to read it before the congregation,

I arrived at my new home in North Carolina on August 21, 2013. On August 30, I joined the Liberty Baptist Church of Durham. I thought I moved to Durham to begin a new life. Looking back, I realize that I moved to Durham to start to grieve. I met some of the dearest Christians on earth that year, but again, most of my memories of that time are just a blur.

## Bottled Tears

I remember that I cried a lot. I walked the North Carolina woods, and I sat on the sun porch in my new home, reading the Bible and praying and wondering what had happened to my life.

I often awoke at night, unable to sleep. I would get on my knees and pray and cry and cry and cry.

I have always been a crybaby. I cry when I am sad, when I am happy and when I am sentimental. I have told my children to ignore me when I cry. I may be a crier, but I dislike pity.

Recently, I was watching a DVD about prayer by Jim Cymbala. I learned that crying is a form of praying, and I was comforted. There were many nights when I tried to pray, and only tears came. I have felt weak, and like I was wasting my time when I could have been getting in touch with God. It was good to realize that weeping can be a way of reaching out to God.

The Bible tells us that God stores our tears in a bottle:

Psalms 56:8, "*Thou tellest my wanderings: put thou my tears into thy bottle: are they not in thy book?*"

I am beginning to understand why God does that. My tears represent my efforts to receive God's help. They symbolize my faith journey with God. Tears are an important part of my learning to commune with the Holy Spirit and to hear His voice. I find hope in God's promise that *"they that sow in tears shall reap in joy"* (Psalm 126:5). I have no doubt that this promise is truth.

## "I Am Pleased With You."

I cannot tell you the exact date, but I heard God's voice in my bedroom in the middle of the night during my first year in North Carolina. I had finally left the "platform" of life behind me. I walked down the street, and no one knew my name or my story. There were no more attorneys, courtrooms, or hearings awaiting. That strange world was in the past. There was nothing left to do but start my life completely over. And all it seemed that I could do was cry and grieve my losses.

I was on my knees by a chair in my bedroom when I heard Someone say, "I am pleased with you." The voice was not audible, but it was indeed the voice of Jesus. Every time that I hear His voice, I am filled with overwhelming joy and peace and a desire to worship Him.

My response to His voice was to cry. I wept and wept and wept. And I am sure that Jesus was weeping with me.

I was amazed. I remember thinking of all the relationship loss I had experienced in the past months. I know that everyone did not walk out on me, but it seemed like they had in those days. I never want to get over the way I felt that night. After all the tears, there was indeed joy and adulation! I was in awe that the One who walked in when everyone else seemed to have walked out was Jesus Christ Himself... And He was pleased. I knew He was pleased. I was overwhelmed.

And again, I was embarrassed. I was ashamed that I had been hard to please. I have been much more tender since that night. I am less likely to judge others. When I heard Jesus' voice that night, He graciously gave me a little extra glimpse of the heart of the Father. I saw a tender heart, one that is easy to please, and I heard a gentle voice.

What did I do to please the Father? Absolutely nothing. That was the point. There was nothing I needed to do. I just reached out with my heart and added little to our two-way conversation but tears—and He said," I am pleased!"

Jesus—the only truly Holy One. Jesus—the Sovereign God. He chose to spend that time with me. Everyone was busy going on with life and rightly so. However, I did not know how to go on with mine. All I had depended on for my reputation, for my righteousness, had seemingly ended in failure, and guess Who had the time to share that messy time with me? I know that it was Jesus—and He was pleased.

## A Miraculous Night

Jesus showed Himself to me in a thousand ways that year, and I perceived His love. Still, there was something different in our relationship after I heard His voice in my darkest hour and learned that He was pleased.

Eventually, I had to decide what to do about my marriage and my future. I was scheduled to go back to Indiana for my son Ken's ordination. God had led him to start a church in West Chester, Ohio, and he was to be ordained just two months after my move to North Carolina. I wanted to be at Ken's ordination, but I was in no way ready to return to Indiana, even for forty-eight hours.

It was October 16, 2013, at 3:00 a.m. I was two months into my year of grieving and crying. I awoke a bit startled and very worried about my trip to Indiiana. I prayed, and I cried and felt like a person feels when they are awake in the middle of the night—a bit fuzzy-headed. Sometime during that nighttime prayer vigil, I heard Jesus' voice like I had never heard it before.

Thoughts ran through my mind that I knew were not my own, They were extremely clear and detailed—so clear that I was able to write them down into nine points. I don't know how to describe it. It was not an audible sound, but I knew that I had heard God's voice. It was the most awesome experience of this journey. I knew from that point on, what God wanted me to do with my future. I have used those nine points as a sort of road map for my journey over the past seven years. I still have my list. In fact, I have it beside me as I write this.

The list of nine points are dated and entitled, "Decisions I made at 3:00 a.m. on 10/16/13."

1.  Don't attack anybody.

2.  Don't defend yourself to anyone.

3.  Move forward and don't look back. There is nothing left of your past.

4.  Don't worry about what anyone thinks. Follow God and move forward.

5.  Quit grieving over what your children have lost. I took it from them, and I have something better for them.

6.  Love God and serve God.

7.  Serve the church and serve people.

8.  All is forgiven—no more guilt and no more shame.

9.  You cannot give your children their life back, but you can be a good example for them.

Every time I have heard God's voice, great joy has followed the experience. I woke the next morning with no more anxiety about the trip ahead. I walked through the airport and traveled to Indiana, grinning as though I were keeping a sensational secret—and I was. God and I had a secret, and we have shared several secrets since then.

God is more magnificent than we can possibly understand. In so many ways, I am learning that He doesn't want me to understand Him; He wants me to trust Him. I have also learned that He loves to share secrets with His children and with His friends. Isn't that what friends do?

The voice of the enemy is full of death and destruction. It evokes confusion and anxiety. I am learning to recognize and avoid listening to that voice.

The voice of Jesus is full of peace and joy, and it evokes love and worship. Since that first time I heard God's voice, I frequently lay in my bed, listening and wanting to hear it again. Sometimes like a giggly child, I ask, "Hey Jesus, would You do that again?"

Other times I just quietly plead, "Please let me hear Your voice."

Since October 16, 2013, Jesus has shown me the way and answered my questions many times in myriad ways. But I don't think I have experienced anything else comparable to hearing His voice on that night. I have doubted many things since then—some things I should not have doubted. But I have never doubted those nine points.

## What Jesus Sounds Like

Let me end this chapter by telling you what Jesus sounds like—to me—in the dark.

1. The voice of Jesus sounds miraculous and truthful. His voice can show you the truth when you have no other way of knowing it.

I Corinthians 2:10, *"But God hath revealed them unto us by his Spirit: for the Spirit searches all things, yea, the deep things of God."*

2. The voice of Jesus sounds tender and gentle and easy to please.

3. The voice of Jesus sounds close.

4. The voice of Jesus is clear. He can guide and show us exactly what to do.

Jesus didn't speak to me with a loud, distant boom. He didn't shoot off a quick email or schedule my time around His. He came with a quiet, peaceful voice, when other voices would not come, or could not come. He was the One Who wasn't too important or too busy...and I was amazed.

I told a pastor friend that I had once believed that God would not speak to a woman without speaking through her husband or a pastor.

He looked at me, puzzled. Now I understand why. There is no one alive for whom my Jesus would not fight to show up in a time of need. When He wants to speak, nothing and no one can keep him silent.

That leads me to the final thing I want to say concerning the voice of Jesus. In the dark, when no one else is there, Jesus' voice is personal. He has secrets just for Cindy and messages only Cindy can hear. That is the kind of voice I need in the dark. And that is the kind of voice Jesus has.

Jesus has secrets just for you, too. He has messages that only you can hear. And He would fight His way to show up for you anywhere, whenever you need Him. That is why I wanted to write this book for you. I want you to listen for and hear His voice. I want you to know what Jesus sounds like—in the dark. If you hear His voice, it will change you, and you will have an experience that cannot be forgotten.

# GLOSSARY OF SCRIPTURES

*Deuteronomy 29:29, "**The secret things belong unto the Lord our God**: but those things which are revealed belong unto us and to our children forever, that we may do all the words of this law."*

*Psalms 16:7, "I will bless the Lord, **who hath given me counsel**, my reins also instruct me in the night seasons."*

*Psalms 17:3a, "Thou hast proved mine heart, **thou hast visited me in the night...**"*

*Psalms 25:14, "**The secret of the Lord is with them that fear him**, and he will shew them his covenant."*

*Proverbs 3:32b, "...but **his secret** is with the righteous."*

*Proverbs 19:21, "There are many devices in a man's heart, nevertheless **the counsel of the Lord, that shall stand.**"*

*Daniel 2:22, "**He revealed the deep and secret things**: he knoweth what is in darkness, and the light dwelleth with him."*

*Daniel 2:47," The king answered unto Daniel, and said, Of a truth it is, that **your God is a God of gods and a Lord of kings, and a revealer of secrets** seeing thou couldest reveal this secret."*

John 10:4, "*And when he putteth forth his own sheep, he goeth before them, and the sheep follow him: **for they know his voice**.*"

John 10:27, "***My sheep hear my voice,** and I know them, and they follow me.*"

John 18:37, "*Every one that is of the truth **heareth my voice**.*"

John 16:13, "*Howbeit, when he, the Spirit of truth is come, he will guide you into all truth, for he shall not speak of himself, but whatsoever, he shall hear, that shall he speak: **and he will shew you things to come**.*"

James 1:5-8, "***If any of you lack wisdom, let him ask of God,** that giveth to all men liberally and upbraideth not, and **it shall be given him.** But let him ask in faith, nothing wavering, For he that wavereth is like a wave of the sea driven with the wind and tossed. For let not that man think that he shall receive anything of the Lord. A double-minded man is unstable in all his ways.*"

# Chapter 5
## A Personal God

*O*n January 3, 2014, I found myself returning home after the holidays. I had celebrated Christmas in my son's home in West Chester, Ohio. After Christmas, I drove to my former home area and spent New Year's Day with friends.

I had booked a flight back to North Carolina on Southwest Airlines. When my friend Janet dropped me off at Chicago Midway Airport, I found the line to check in at Southwest to be winding through the lobby and into a back hallway. Before I got to the back of the line, I saw a sign that said the wait time was 2 hours. I was dragging too much luggage with me (which my children will tell you is typical) and the thought of standing in line for two hours by myself was overwhelming. And so I made an "Executive Decision." I spent another $400 to purchase a Delta flight and I "scrapped" the flight on Southwest. I was able to walk right up to the ticket agent, purchase my ticket and go to my gate. About an hour later, I found myself in Seat 17F on Delta Flight 500. It was a window seat.

I recall being overwhelmed at the thought that no one in the world knew where I was. "If the plan crashed," I wondered, "how long would it be, before someone would even know I was missing?" Those are morbid thoughts, I know, but not unusual thoughts for a recently forsaken spouse.

I was born and raised in the home of a very traditional mother. I often say that she was the "1st coming of Martha Stewart." Born in 1959, I probably took for granted that my mother was so present in my life. She was both a domestic goddess and a predictable presence. The television show "Father Knows Best" was still airing during my childhood. The perfect mother, June Cleaver, had nothing on my mother.

I never wondered if breakfast would be ready in the morning, if my lunch would be packed, or if dinner would be on the table -promptly at 5:00 pm–I might add. I threw my dirty clothes into a laundry chute that took them straight to the washer and dryer in the basement, and they somehow miraculously ended up folded and back in my drawers in no time–every time. Most of my school years, even during high school, my mom chose to pick me up from school. And whether or not she picked me up, she was almost never missing when I arrived home.

I was the youngest of four children, and by the time I was about to leave the nest, our large church had become a mega church. My mother was a bit of a "celebrity" in our Christian world. Still she usually excused herself from whatever meeting she might be attending, because "Cindy will be coming home from school."

I had a father who traveled every week. He left, almost like clockwork, every Monday morning and arrived back from his speaking engagement every Wednesday afternoon. Even so, he sat down with us every morning he was in town to share a hot breakfast (in a shirt and tie), and he arrived home every night promptly at 5:00 p.m, for family dinner. He would often return to work after dinner, and he was gone a lot, but he was the kind of dad who, when he was present he was truly "present."

He was also a very strong dad. To illustrate how strong he was, he and my future fiancé decided when we would become engaged and chose the wedding date. They also picked out our first house together. I saw what it looked like after it had been purchased. All of that did not even seem strange to me until decades later.

I left my father and mother's home when I got married; I was just 19. I had only lived in one house up until after my honeymoon. Then I was married for almost 35 years. Needless to say, I was not used to making very many "Executive decisions." Now all decisions were my decisions.

Now I was 10,000 miles up in the air, and no one knew where I was. Dad had passed away years earlier, Mom was living alone in

Dallas, Texas, my children and grandchildren were with other family finishing their holiday celebration, and my husband was in prison. The loneliness was terrible–there is a loneliness that feels like it can kill you. I experienced that loneliness many times during those first years as a forsaken wife.

I am always reminded of that day when I read Psalm 139:7-10,

> *"Whither shall I go from thy spirit? Or whither shall I flee from thy presence? If I ascend up into heaven, thou art there: if I make my bed in hell, behold, thou art there. If I take the wings of the morning, and dwell in the uttermost parts of the sea; Even there shall thy hand lead me, and thy right hand shall hold me."*

Because I realized that no one knew where I was, I took special note of my flight and seat number–something I am guilty of NOT doing on most flights. I usually prefer an aisle seat, but in my assigned seat that day, I found myself looking out the window.

## A Horizontal Rainbow

While I gazed, with tears in my eyes, I saw something I had never seen before. I saw a rainbow above the clouds. It was not an arched rainbow; it was a perfectly stacked rainbow. Layers of every color of the rainbow were piled ever so neatly on top of the clouds. And I remembered Jesus' promise in Isaiah 54:10, and his "covenant of peace."

> *"For this is as the waters of Noah unto me: for as I have sworn that the waters of Noah should no more go over the earth...neither shall the covenant of my peace be removed..."*

Verses 11 and 12 go on to say,

*"O thou afflicted, tossed with tempest, and not comforted, behold, I will lay thy stones with fair colors, and lay thy foundations with sapphires. And I will make thy windows of agates and thy gates of carbuncles, and all thy borders of pleasant stones."*

Just as God used the rainbow in Noah's day, God once again uses the colors of the rainbow to describe the covenant that He has made with His children–only this time they seem to be described in layers. I imagine they describe what the gates in Heaven might look like.

On January 3, 2014, I once again heard the voice of God. As I looked over at that beautiful layered rainbow, I knew that God was making a covenant with me.

If you should turn in my Bible to Psalms 111:5, you would see these words,

*He hath given meat unto them that fear him; HE WILL EVER BE MINDFUL OF HIS COVENANT."*

And in the margin you will see: "**1/3/14 Window Seat–Delta Flt.500–Seat 17F**"

I believe with all of my heart that God made a covenant with me that day–in that seat, on that flight. Someone was very cognizant of my exact whereabouts that day–that Someone was Jesus. If I had waited two hours in that Southwest line, I would not have been where I was supposed to be. That realization was such a comfort to me. And so is the covenant...

Knowing that God and I have a covenant has carried me through seven of the loneliest years of my life. No one knows the covenant–I don't even understand all of it myself. Not all of that covenant has come to pass; some may not come to pass this side of Heaven. But I believe that much of it will come to pass on this earth.

God did not make a covenant with me because I am special. God made a covenant with me because Jesus is special. That is what I want you to know.

I am not sure where the quote originated that says, "God never uses someone greatly without first hurting them deeply," but I believe that to be true. I believe that God will use my sorrow, not because of who I am, but because of Who Jesus is. He has a purpose for all of us and for all of our suffering–we just have to let Him direct our steps. We have to be in the right seat at the right time. And we need to be aware that it is Jesus doing the directing and not we ourselves.

## God made a covenant with Noah,

*"But with thee I will establish a covenant;"* Gen.6:18.

Genesis 9:9, *"And I, behold, I establish my covenant with you, and with your seed after you."*

Genesis 9:11, *"And I will establish my covenant with you..."*

Genesis 9:13, 16, 17, *"I do set my bow in the cloud, and it shall be for a token of a covenant between me and the earth. And it shall come to pass, when I bring a cloud over the earth, that the bow shall be seen in the cloud. And the bow shall be in the cloud, and I will look upon it, that I may remember the everlasting covenant between God and every living creature of all flesh that is upon the earth. And God said unto Noah, This is the TOKEN of the covenant, which I have established between me and all flesh that is upon earth."*

The rainbow is a token of God's covenant to Noah and of salvation by grace.

The rainbow is one of the many tokens of the covenant between God and me.

**God made a covenant with Abraham,**

> Genesis 15:18, *"In the same day the Lord made a covenant with Abram, saying, Unto thy seed have I given this land."*

> Genesis 17:11b, *"...and it shall be a token of the covenant betwixt you and me."* (This token was circumcision, and I think I like the rainbow token better.)

**God made a covenant with Isaac,**

> Genesis 17:21, *"But my covenant will I establish with Isaac, which Sarah shall bear unto thee at this set time in the next year."*

**God made a covenant with David,**

> Psalm 89:3, *"I made a covenant with my chosen, I have sworn unto David my servant."*

All throughout the Bible, we see God making covenants with his children—with Joseph it was a dream.

**God remembered His covenant to the Children of Israel,**

> Exodus 2:24, *"And God heard their groaning, and God remembered his covenant..."*

Not only does God make covenants with His people, but the covenants of God are personal, as are the tokens of those covenants. God even calls the plagues that He performed in Egypt "tokens." Jesus is a personal God, and He uses personal things to display His love and His covenant to His children.

Jesus has used personal tokens such as rainbows, sunsets, and butterflies, to comfort me in recent years. He has definitely used His Word and music to remind me of His covenant with me. And His covenants are indeed personal,

**His covenant with Noah was personal:**

> Genesis 9 :12, "*And God said, This is the token of the covenant which I make between me and you.*"

> Genesis 9:15, "*And I will remember my covenant, which is between me and you...*"

**His covenant with Abraham was personal,**

> Genesis 7:2, "*And I will make my covenant between me and thee and will multiply thee exceedingly.*"

> Genesis 7:4, "*As for me, behold, my covenant is with thee...*"

> Genesis 7:7, "*And I will establish my covenant between me and thee...*"

> Genesis 7:10, "*This is my covenant, which ye shall keep, between me and you and thy seed after thee...;*"

**God's covenant with me is personal.** I don't understand it; I don't deserve it, but I have a "you and me" kind of relationship with God.

It is not a "thee and thou" relationship.
It is not a God and the world relationship.
It is a "me and you" relationship.
It is a Jesus and Cindy relationship.

And I am sharing my story because I want you to know—if you don't already—that same kind of personal relationship is available to you—whoever you are, and whatever you've done, or however you've failed and/or however life seems to have failed you.

Depending on what part of the country in which you live, it is a covenant between "y'all," or "you guys."

As stated earlier in this chapter, I have not seen all of my covenant fulfilled, nor do I understand all of it, but for the seven toughest years of my life, I have lived in hope—because of a covenant—a personal covenant between my friend Jesus—Him—and me. Daily I watch for the tokens of those covenants and He is faithful, and I see His hand—and I see His love.

Perhaps not all of that covenant will be fulfilled this side of Heaven, but someday I will enter Heaven, and I will pass those pearly gates and those walls, layered with precious rainbow colored stones,

Revelation 21:19,20 "*And the foundations of the wall of the city were garnished with all manner of precious stones. The first foundation was jasper; the second sapphire; the third, a chalcedony; the fourth, an emerald; the sixth, sardius, the seventh, chrysolite; the eighth, beryl, the ninth, a topaz; the tenth, a chrysoprasus, the eleventh, a jacinth, the twelfth, an amethyst.*"

And I will stand before my Jesus—him and me.

I used to think that I would ask him "Why?" when I see Him. Why would all of "this" and "that" happen to a good little Sunday school girl? But I doubt I will. I think I will fall at His feet in true humility, finally, and I think I will know. I will know that the covenant has been fulfilled–the covenant between Jesus and me. And everywhere there will be rainbows and tokens–to remind me.

I will know–and I will look at His face–and into His eyes–and into His heart–and "why" won't matter.

# GLOSSARY OF SCRIPTURE

*Leviticus 26;9, "For I will have respect unto you, and make you fruitful, and multiply you, and establish my **covenant** with you."*

*Deuteronomy 5:3, "The Lord made not this **covenant** with our fathers, but with us..."*

*I Kings 8:23, "And he said, Lord God of Israel, there is no God like thee, in heaven above, or on earth beneath, who keepest **covenant** and mercy with thy servants that walk before thee with all their heart."*

*II Chronicles 6:14, "And said, O Lord God of Israel, there is no God like thee in the heaven, nor in the earth; which keepest **covenant**, and shewest mercy unto thy servants, that walk before thee with all their hearts."*

*Psalms 25:15, "The secret of the Lord is with them that fear him; and he will shew them his **covenant**."*

*Psalms 89:28, "My mercy will I keep for him forevermore, and my **covenant** shall stand fast with him.:*

*Psalms 89:34, "My **covenant** will I not break, nor alter the thing that is gone out of my lips."*

*Psalms 105:8,9,10 "He hath remembered his **covenant** forever, the word which he commanded to a thousand generations. Which **covenant** he* *made with Abraham, and his oath unto Isaac. And confirmed the same unto Jacob for a law, and to Israel for an everlasting **covenant**."*

*Psalms 106:45, "And he remembered for them his **covenant**..."*

*Psalms 111:9, "He sent redemption unto his people: he hath commanded his **covenant** forever: holy and reverend is his name."*

*Jeremiah 33:20,21, "Thus saith the Lord; if ye can break my **covenant** of the day, and my **covenant** of the night, and that there should not be day and night in their season. Then may also my **covenant** be broken with David my servant, that he should not have a son to reign upon his throne; and with the Levites the priests, my ministers."*

*Jeremiah 33:25, "Thus saith the Lord, If my **covenant** be not with day and night, and if I have not appointed the ordinances of heaven and earth."*

# Chapter 6
## A Lesson on Humility

*O*ne of the most challenging parts of my journey in the past seven years has been finding a job and supporting myself for the first time. Since high school, I had worked jobs for one ministry or another in my home church. After thirty years of serving in several capacities, I was left without retirement and few transferable skills.

I had to start completely over, and I was frightened. A friend suggested I get a job at a nearby retirement village. I applied and was quickly accepted. I was excited. It felt like I was finally taking a step forward in my new life. I knew I could not support myself sitting on the sun porch and walking the North Carolina woods.

Right after I was hired, I learned that my boss would not be able to keep me busy unless I went to school and became a Certified Nurses' Assistant. I was a bit naive about what this position was all about. I didn't understand why I had not been told about the requirement before I was hired.

I walked straight out of my boss's office and drove to a small school that had a fast-track program for certification. For six weeks, I worked part-time and attended school. After completing my training, I took my first exam and failed. On the second try, I passed and became a CNA.

I supported myself with this job. It paid $11.00 an hour. I picked up a lot of overtime and sometimes worked between 55 and 60 hours a week. I was able to pay for my townhouse and live a comfortable life, as well as a very busy one,

As a CNA, I was assigned various shifts, and I had several types of clients. I worked in the independent section for elderly folks who barely needed any help at all. I also worked in the Alzheimer's unit and in the campus hospital.

I honestly needed those clients. While I was grieving the loss of my marriage, God gave me people to nurture. The retirement village was a beautiful and safe place to work. I have fond memories of pushing wheelchairs across the campus and walking around the lake with the clients. There were sweet conversations while I sat with patients on benches beside the water.

Some days I sat most of the day in solitude at the bedside of a semi-comatose patient whose children just wanted someone to watch over them while they slept. I could walk into the hospital room of a patient I had never met and almost instantly tell if the patient was a Christian, even if they slept the entire day. There is just something different about the atmosphere when a dying saint is in the room.

I have run down the street after Alzheimer's patients who sneaked out of the house regularly. I have picked up people twice my weight to place them in their wheelchairs and put them back into their recliners. I have given sponge baths, changed many Depends, and stood outside the shower to assist a resident who needed cleaning up.

I have knelt down and washed feet, dried between toes, and put on compression hose–a feat that involves quite a bit of struggle and requires a particular technique, I might add. Though I felt the stark contrast between my present life and my former one, I did not doubt who I was. I knew who I was. I was a person who was deeply loved and valued by God, and I knew that I always would be.

Two years before, much of my "job" included public appearances where I gave autographs and had my picture taken. I had never enjoyed that part of the job. Instead, I wanted to serve and missed the opportunity. Now, I had the chance. I had plenty of time to serve.

I was sometimes lonely when I finished an 11:00 p.m. shift. I walked to my car to drive home to my townhouse. I can also honestly say that I was at peace and even happy during much of that time.

There was never a time when Jesus was not right beside me. I never washed a foot or dried between toes without feeling His help. He aided me in every compression hose struggle, and I felt it.

I often thought about the story in John 13:3-5: *"Jesus knowing that the Father had given all things into his hands and that he was come from God, and went to God. He riseth from supper and laid aside his garments, and took a towel, and girded himself. After that, he poureth water into a basin and began to wash the disciples' feet and to wipe them with the towel wherewith he was girded."*

Later, Jesus rebukes Peter for refusing to allow the Lord to wash his feet. He spoke these words in verses 14 and 15 of chapter 13: *"If I then, your Lord and Master have washed your feet, ye also ought to wash one another's feet. For I have given you an example, that ye should do as I have done to you."*

And verse 17 is one I love, *"If ye know these things, happy are ye if ye do them."*

I have heard people say that God wants us to be holy, not happy; He gives us joy, but not happiness. I believe God does indeed want us to be holy, and I know that He gives a deep abiding joy that is not as fleeting as happiness. But I am also comforted by the fact that the Bible gives us several examples of how to be happy.

I was tired and lonely in those days, but I often left the retirement center just downright happy. The circumstances could be unpleasant, but I realized that I was working alongside Jesus. I felt His presence there and knew that I was serving as unto Him.

## A Change Of Attitude

However, one Friday night, alone in my townhouse, my attitude was completely different. I was probably exhausted, though that was no excuse. I began to yell out my frustrations and take them out on God. I listened to a lot of music to get me through those nights alone, and I still do. That Friday night, however, while the music played about the love and faithfulness of God, I screamed to God, "YOU DON'T LOVE ME! AND YOU ARE NOT FAITHFUL!" It was a long tirade of insults, and I suppose if you could lose your salvation, I would have lost mine that night. The grief and the loneliness became too heavy for me. I fell asleep exhausted and woke the next morning, numb.

It was Saturday morning, and I had to work with a lady named Bonnie. As I prepared to go to work, I thought that I should apologize to God, but some bitterness had set in, and I did not apologize. I was still numb, and I was still offended.

Bonnie was a sweet and gentle lady who would come and go mentally because she was in the early stages of dementia. We sat side by side in her living room that day, and she was unusually cognizant. I felt such love for her. I had not premeditated this, but I began to tell Bonnie about Jesus, and she accepted Him as her Savior that day.

My shift was over just after noon, and I drove home. While in the car, I was puzzled, and I said to Jesus, "So that is what You are going to do to me after the way I treated You last night. You are going to let me lead someone to You?"

I had already witnessed to many people in my life. I led my first person to Christ when I was a young girl sitting with a neighbor friend on my front lawn. I have seen many saved since, and each soul saved felt like a reward from God for my good behavior. When I witnessed to someone, and they did not get saved, I assumed that I had somehow evoked God's displeasure. So much of my life was steeped in trying to earn that which was completely out of reach.

The Lord answered my previous question in the car that day. He didn't speak out loud, but He spoke clearly. He said:

*"Cindy, none of the people you have ever won to Christ were about you. They were all about my mercy."*

I wept, and I was no longer numb. I gave Jesus a great, big "I'm sorry." I was genuinely repentant. Somehow, I knew that I was forgiven even before I had spewed those ugly words out of my mouth the night before. In fact, I had been forgiven thousands of years earlier, when Jesus cried, "It is finished," on Calvary's cross. I drove home that day not as a pastor's wife, but as a CNA—a servant. I was enveloped in the mercy of God. I was completely forgiven, and I was happy.

On another occasion, I shared Christ with one of the sweetest ladies on earth. Mary was the widow of a man who had been part of the leadership of a very liberal religious organization. Mary and I would often sit and chat. This was a part of my job that I loved very much. I cared about Mary, and she cared about me. On one ordinary morning in the life of this CNA, Mary bowed her head and accepted Jesus as her Savior.

As I drove home that morning, I thought of all the members I had left behind at my home megachurch. I thought of all the plans that had to be made and all I had to go through to get to Mary so I could tell her about Jesus that day. And I remembered God's words:

> John 15:4-7: *"What man of you, having an hundred sheep, if he lose one of them, doth not leave the ninety and nine in the wilderness, and go after that which is lost, until he find it? And when he hath found it, he layeth it on his shoulders, rejoicing. And when he cometh home, he calleth together his friends and neighbors, saying unto them, Rejoice with me; for I have found my sheep which was lost, I say unto you, that likewise, joy shall be in heaven over one sinner that repenteth, more than over ninety and nine just persons, which need no repentance."*

I told many co-workers and precious patients about Jesus in that nursing home. I knelt down, not to pray, but to wash feet, to put on compression hose, and to serve as unto Jesus. It was a humble ministry, but it was our ministry together—mine and His.

I heard many of those valuable people pray to accept Jesus as their Savior—one lost sheep at a time. Each time I did, I knew that heaven was happy and that Jesus was happy—and despite the circumstances, I was happy too.

*A Lesson On Humility*

# GLOSSARY OF SCRIPTURE

*Deuteronomy 8:16, "Who fed thee in the wilderness with manna, which thy fathers knew not, that he might **humble** thee, and that he might prove thee, to do thee good at thy latter end."*

*II Chronicles 7:14, "If my people, which are called by my name, shall **humble** themselves, and pray, and seek my face, and turn from their wicked ways; then will I hear from heaven, and will forgive their sin, and will heal their land."*

*II Chronicles 34:27, "Because thine heart was tender, and thou didst **humble** thyself before God, when thou heardest his words against this place, and against the inhabitants thereof, and **humbledst** thyself before me, and didst rend thy clothes, and weep before me; I have even heard thee also, saith the Lord."*

*Job 22:29, "When men are cast down, then thou shalt say, There is lifting up, and he shall save the **humble** person."*

*Proverbs 16:19, "Better it is to be of a **humble** spirit with the lowly, than to divide the spoil with the proud."*

*Proverbs 22:4, "By **humility** and the fear of the Lord are riches and honour, and life."*

*Proverbs 29;23, "A man's pride shall bring him low, but honor shall uphold the **humble** in spirit."*

*Matthew 23:12, "And whosoever shall exalt himself shall be abased; and he that shall **humble** himself shall be exalted."*

*James 4:6, "But he giveth more grace, Wherefore he saith, God resisteth the proud, but giveth grace unto the **humble**."*

*James 4:10, "**Humble** yourselves in the sight of the Lord, and he shall lift you up."*

*I Peter 5:5c, "...for God resisteth the proud, and giveth grace unto the **humble.**"*

*I Peter 5:6, "**Humble** yourselves therefore under the mighty hand of God, that he may exalt you in due time."*

# Chapter 7
## "Grace is a Scary Thing"

*O*n May 28, 2014, my divorce went through. It was a crazy time for a marriage to end–three days before what would have been our 35th wedding anniversary. On our 25<sup>th</sup> anniversary, we had renewed our vows. Our children had planned the ceremony in the back yard of a lovely Victorian home. It was a perfectly beautiful day, and the venue reminded me of the wedding that took place in the movie, "Father of the Bride." I never imagined that our marriage would be over ten years later.

May I say that I believe wholly in the sanctity of marriage. I also believe that God, in His grace, placed an exception clause in His Word. It was not my first desire to utilize that exception. I do not wish to share the details of my decision to divorce, nor do I wish to defend myself. I just want to state that to me, there was no other option.

I took nearly two years to decide to divorce. As awful as this may sound, I was relieved when the process was over. It took longer, however, to let go of the regret of the loss.

As 2014 ended, and I began to look towards 2015, I felt a strong need to change churches. I had met some of the sweetest folks in the world at Liberty Baptist Church of Durham, North Carolina. Part of me would have loved to grow old with these dear people. However, I felt a tug to find a place where I could grieve and worship in private–where no one knew me.

A friend mentioned the strong Bible teaching of Pastor Stephen Davey. As I was praying about where to go to church, I had two other acquaintances mention how they loved to hear Stephen preach on his radio program, Wisdom for the Heart. I looked on the Website of the Colonial Baptist Church of Cary, NC, where Stephen pastors. I was impressed.

I believe it was the first Sunday after my divorce when I visited Colonial. I stayed at Colonial for five years. Week after week, God met me there. Stephen and his wife Marsha reached out to me a bit, and I was blessed to experience the grace and humility of their lives and ministry. I had a few conversations with them about the changes that were taking place in my heart. It was at Colonial under Stephen Davey's teaching that I learned to appreciate this idea that "Grace is a scary thing."

Attending a church where no one knew my story, I felt a freedom I had not felt before. The peer pressure of the "fear of man" seemed like an echo from my past. I fell in love with the praying people and the Bible teaching church that God and I had chosen.

One of the outreaches of the Colonial Baptist Church is a ministry called Divorce Care. This is a recovery support group where you can find help and healing for the hurt of separation and divorce. (divorce-care.org) I attended Divorce care for about four months. For nearly ten weeks, every Wednesday evening, after a long day of work at the retirement village, I made the forty-minute drive to church, sat in a small Sunday school room where I watched a DVD and cried and shared with other heartbroken divorcees. Most of them were much younger than I was. The program was led by two couples who had been divorced and remarried. Their compassion was a gift from God to us.

The hosting of such a ministry can be a hassle to a local church. Some might feel that such an outreach condones divorce. For me, Divorce Care was a lifeline. Several who attended did not go to any church and were unbelievers. I had the privilege of leading a Catholic school teacher to the Lord while we attended Divorce Care together. She and I still keep in touch, and she is now a faithful attendee at Colonial.

It is hard to explain the pain of divorce to someone who has never been through it. All pain is difficult, and I don't mean to elevate the pain of the divorcee above any other heartache. But divorce is the death of a one flesh relationship. In my case, it was also the death of my family as I had known it. I needed to take time to cry and grieve. I am so grateful to have found a place to do that, amid believers and under the sound of their Biblical advice.

## Divorce And Forgiveness

One of the subjects that we discussed in Divorce Care is the subject of forgiveness. In 2012, I wrote two letters to two people whose actions had drastically changed my life and the lives of my children and grand-children. In one letter, I apologized for any hurt that had taken place. I was not responsible for that hurt, and yet I knew that an essential part of my healing would be to express my sympathy.

In the second letter, I expressed forgiveness to another individual. This person did not ask my forgiveness. I did not receive a response from either letter. Seven years later, I am at peace with the fact that I took the time early on to say, "I'm sorry for your hurt," and "I forgive."

## Hurt By Strangers

When I read about the story of the four Hebrew children who were taken captive in Babylon, Daniel, Shadrach, Meshach, and Abednego, I see that I am not the first person whose life was entirely altered by the lives of others. These young men were taken from their home, their home area, and their families to work as servants for the strangers in Babylon. They even had their names changed. Their entire life was stripped from them. And what was their response?

Bitterness toward God? No, Daniel still prayed 3 times every day, and Shadrach, Meschach, and Abednego walked through fire, rather than turn their back on their God. All three men came out of the fire, and, as the Bible says, they didn't even smell like smoke. Daniel came out of the lions' den without even a scratch or a tooth mark. The Bible says the lions didn't even open their mouths while Daniel was near them.

The actions of people had no effect on the faith of Daniel and the others. The actions of people altered the circumstances of their lives, but their attitudes were unchanged.

A few years ago, I sat across from a client where I worked and saw the bitterness on her face. She was struggling with her health, but I could tell that the struggle went deeper than that. I probed a little, and she began to talk. "I was divorced fourteen years ago, and you don't understand the effect it had on me. I just can't get over what was done to my children."

I did not bother to tell her that I did understand. I simply shared with her about Jesus–the One who understands everything about her. She was a Christian, and I believe she was helped by our conversation that day. That day, I saw on her face what I do not want to become. Every day I have a choice whether or not I will become a bitter person. Writing this book won't end my struggle in that area. The only thing that will fight off that bitterness is a daily dose of forgiveness.

In my heart, before God, daily, I ask Him to forgive me for every time I have hurt someone in my life. I have hurt so many throughout these years–hopefully, unintentionally most of the time. But I have been hurtful, nonetheless.

I tell Jesus every morning that in my heart before Him, I forgive everyone who has hurt me.

## A Tender Heart

Ephesians 4:32, "*And be ye kind one to another, tenderhearted, forgiving one another, even as God for Christ's sake hath forgiven you.*"

I once heard Pastor Bobby Roberson, now in Heaven, give a brief devotional on that verse. As I recall, he taught it backward.

1. Unforgiveness leads to hard-heartedness.

2. Hardheartedness leads to unkindness.

I forgive daily to keep my heart tender. Many divorced women wear a hard expression that seems to reveal an even harder heart. God, in His grace, has allowed me to keep a tender heart. I value that tender heart as a precious gift. And I guard it.

The repercussions of your hurts and mine will not completely dissipate this side of Heaven. The scars remain. Because of this, forgiveness must be a daily choice and practice.

I also forgive, so that I might remain kind. How do people do such atrocious things to other people? I believe it starts with unforgiveness. I am capable of those things, and so are you. Therefore, we must guard our tender hearts with the powerful weapon of forgiveness and, even more so, with the grace of our kindhearted Savior, Jesus.

I forgive, but not because I am a "good little Sunday school girl." I forgive because of Who Jesus is. The same grace that allows you and me the freedom to follow God's Word rather than the fear of man is the same grace the allows us to free ourselves from the actions of others. That grace allows us to relinquish control over the behavior of people.

## Freedom Of Grace

I used to think of "freedom" as a rebellious word–a liberal word. But true freedom is simply the grace to follow God and His Word rather than man. One of the greatest freedoms is to look in our hearts and find the grace to forgive, rather than cultivating bitterness there.

## Sovereignty Of God

I forgive because I believe in the Sovereignty of God. God has allowed all of the events of my life over which I had no control. He allowed Daniel to be thrown into the lions' den, but He also allowed the lions' mouths to stay shut. God allowed the three Hebrew boys to be cast into the fiery furnace, but he also left them unburned and smelling more like Febreze than a fire.

God allowed every circumstance of my life so far. He also has extended the grace to forgive. That grace was paid for at Calvary when a tenderhearted Jesus spoke, ***"Father, forgive them for they know not what they do."***

Grace is indeed a scary thing. Through grace, we give people permission to exercise their freedom, even if it hurts us. But grace, while we are holding the hand of God, can ignite miracles. The biggest miracle is one that takes place in our hearts, and that is the miracle of forgiveness.

That is what I received from Jesus in the dark. He extended His hand of grace. I took that grace, and with it came the miracle of forgiveness.

*"Grace is a Scary Thing"*

# GLOSSARY OF SCRIPTURE

*Psalms 95:7,8, "For he is our God, and we are the people of his pasture, and the sheep of his hand. Today. If ye will hear his voice, **Harden not your heart**, as in the provocation, and as in the day of temptation in the wilderness."*

*Proverbs 28:14, "Happy is the man that feareth always; but he that **hardeneth his heart** shall fall into mischief."*

*Matthew 6:14,15, "For if ye **forgive** men their trespasses, your heavenly Father will also **forgive** you: But if ye **forgive** not men their trespasses, neither will your Father **forgive** your trespasses."*

*Mark 11:25,26, "And when ye stand praying, **forgive**, if ye have ought against any: that your Father also which is in heaven may **forgive** you your trespasses. But if ye do not **forgive**, neither will your Father which is in heaven **forgive** your trespasses."*

*Luke 6:37, "**Judge** not, and ye shall not be **judged**: condemn not, and ye shall not be condemned: **forgive**, and ye shall be **forgiven**."*

*Luke 17:3,4, "Take heed to yourselves; If thy brother trespass against thee, rebuke him; and if he repents, **forgive** him. And if he trespass against thee seven times in a day, and seven times in a day turn again to thee, saying, I repent; thou shalt **forgive** him."*

*John 12:40, "He hath blinded their eyes, and **hardened their heart**; that they should not see with their eyes, nor understand with their heart, and be converted, and I should heal them."*

*Romans 14:10, "But why dost thou **judge** thy brother: or why dost thou set at nought thy brother? For we shall all stand before the judgment seat of Christ."*

*I Thessalonians 5:15, "See that none render evil for evil unto any man; but ever follow that which is good, both among yourselves, and to all men."*

*Hebrews 3:7,8, "Wherefore (as the Holy Ghost saith, Today if ye will hear his voice, **harden not your hearts**, as in the provocation., in the day of temptation in the wilderness.*

*Hebrews 3:13, "But exhort one another daily, while it is called Today; lest any of you be **hardened** through the deceitfulness of sin."*

*Hebrews 3:15, "While it is said, Today if ye will hear his voice, **harden not your hearts**, as in the provocation."*

*James 4:11,12, "Speak not evil one of another, brethren. He that speaketh evil of his brother and **judgeth** his brother, speaketh evil of the law, and **judgeth** the law: but if thou **judge** the law, thou art not a doer of the law, but a **judge**. There is one lawgiver, who is able to save and to destroy, who art thou that **judgest** another?"*

# Chapter 8
## Children of Divorce

*I*n March of 2016, my daughter, Jaclynn, told me that she and Todd would be moving away from North Carolina. I had moved to NC because of them, and now they were leaving. Todd had taken a position in Temperance, Michigan. They waited till the end of the school year, and, in early June, they sold their home in Durham, packed up their belongings, and moved back to the Midwest.

It sounds terrible, but I was both relieved and sad to see them go. I recall standing at the front of my townhouse, watching them drive away. I waved at my daughter, son-in-law, and four of my grandchildren until they were out of sight. It was a sad moment.

I was still grieving deeply, and I was busy working overtime at the retirement village. My kids and I had been attending different churches in NC. We didn't let that come between us, but it felt awkward at times.

Right after their departure, I planned a trip to see my son, Ken, and his wife and children in Ohio. I packed my things and my puppy and took the scenic 10-hour drive through North Carolina, the Virginia mountains, West Virginia, and to West Chester, Ohio–a lovely suburb of Cincinnati, where Ken and his family live.

I stayed a week and then drove back to Durham, where I would live for the first time, with no family anywhere nearby. I loved my children dearly–I believe as much as any mother possibly could, but I just felt so useless at that time.

I was alone in NC for three years, and I carried four children and seven grandchildren in my heart every second of those years. I texted them every morning, and I still do that to this day–not because I am needy–but because I need them to know that I am always "here" for them, even when I am far away.

Across the hallway from the small room where I met for Divorce Care, another group called Divorce Care for Kids met. This is a divorce recovery group to help children, 5-12 years of age, heal from the pain caused by a separation or divorce. (dc4k.org) This group was comprised of little children, who met with some compassionate ladies, to learn how much Jesus loves them and also how to cope with their parents' divorce. My heart went out to those children.

Even though my children were adults when their parents divorced, my heart went out to them as well. They had to start completely over, after living in the same area and attending the same megachurch all of their lives.

My kids have said they think I grieved for them more than I grieved for myself, and I did grieve deeply. No mother brings her baby home from the hospital and wishes to give them the life they were handed in July of 2012. Perhaps it is vain thinking, but I believe all parents want their children to be proud of them.

My granddaughter, Lexy, now eleven years old, has sometimes been called my "mini-me." Something about her personality does remind me of myself as a child. I remember looking at her just after Jack left, and thinking, "I hope her life doesn't turn out like mine." Those feelings sometimes overwhelmed me, especially when our family life had seemed perfectly happy for so many years.

Genesis 21 records the flight of the first single mother, Hagar. She is in the wilderness and running from her Master Abraham (He was also the father of her son Ishmael) and his extremely livid wife, Sarah.

Hagar has nothing to offer her son, so she just sets him down and begins to cry.

Genesis 21:17 says, "*And God heard the voice of the lad, and the angel of God called to Hagar out of heaven and said unto her, What aileth thee, Hagar? Fear not, FOR GOD HATH HEARD THE VOICE OF THE LAD WHERE HE IS.*"

In my Bible beside that verse, I have written, "God hears the sorrow of Jaclynn and Ken."

My first Father's Day alone really caught me off guard. It was the most challenging holiday of all. I don't mean to belittle my children's father–that is definitely not the purpose of this book. But I was so comforted that God was willing to take the Father role for my children. I was so grateful that he could hear their cries–and I know there were many.

I am also thankful for my children's spouses. They have comforted me so much by displaying such love and commitment to my children while they were hurting, and as they have been rebuilding their lives.

Birth children are born out of sorrow and travail, and Jaclynn and Ken are the dearest birth children a mother can ask for. So many times, I have complained to the Lord about all I lost, and He has reminded me that my children's faith is still intact. My reply has always been, "You are right, Lord. (And, of course, He is.) I really haven't lost anything."

If birth children are born out of sorrow and travail, then my son-in-law Todd and my daughter-in-law Candace have become like birth children to me. We have endured much sorrow and travail together, and they have genuinely loved my children. Though they have wonderful parents of their own, I never think about having two children–I have four, and I am so pleased with all of them.

I realize they will continue to struggle until they reach Heaven, as we all do and will. But I am so privileged to have my four children as a part of my life. I know they have cried buckets of tears, and they have been nurtured through it by our Heavenly Father–the greatest Father of all.

For those who work in any way with the children of divorce–I thank you. You are doing the work of the Heavenly Father. And to those who seek to do God's work in His churches, please don't forget to care about the children of divorce–no matter what their age.

James 1:27, *"Pure religion and undefiled before God and the Father is this, to visit the fatherless and widows in their affliction, and to keep himself unspotted from the world."*

Genesis 21:20 says, *"And God was with the lad, and he grew and dwelt in the wilderness."*

I love that Ishmael grew to be an archer–a manly man–even though he was at least for some time raised without his father.

I love that God took the time to be with the child of the first single mother.

If you want to know Jesus better, I know where you can find Him. You will see him in the wilderness of divorce, hanging out with the children of divorce.

Jesus won't be mad at them; He won't be judging them; He will be loving them. He genuinely cares about their wellbeing. Jesus will be their Father.

If you want to find Jesus in the dark, among the children of divorce is one place I am sure that you will find Him.

# GLOSSARY OF SCRIPTURE

*Psalms 10:14c, "thou art the helper of the **fatherless**."*

*Psalms 68:5, "A **fathe**r of the **fatherless**, and a judge of the widows, is God in his holy habitation."*

*Psalms 82:3, "Defend the poor and **fatherless**: do justice to the afflicted and needy."*

*Psalms 146:9, "The Lord preserveth the strangers; he relieveth the **fatherless** and widow..."*

# Chapter 9
## Pure Religion

*D*uring the past seven years, I have continually learned that timing is everything with God. He knows how to make a way when it seems there is none. Jesus and His Holy Spirit can move mountains. I saw Him working when I was driving through the Virginia mountains on my way home from visiting Ken and Candace.

It was June of 2016, and I was returning to Durham, to live alone in North Carolina for the first time. My cell phone rang, and it was Bridget. Bridget is one of the strongest and most tenderhearted ladies I have ever known. I don't feel it is my place to tell her story in this book, but it is one of grace and redemption.

Bridget had visited me in NC, and she had offered me a job a couple of times. I had turned down her offers. When I answered her call this time, she offered me a job again. The timing could not have been better. Sometimes you just know in your heart that a call is from God, and I knew it that day. I accepted Bridget's offer, and I began working for her on August 30, 2016.

When I was a pastor's wife, I recall thinking that, if I weren't in ministry, I would enjoy working in nutrition. I had forgotten that wish, but God obviously did not.

I continued to work at the retirement village part-time, but I was growing weary. My new job as a Health Coach allowed me to cut back on physical labor. I also spent less time around the sick and dying, and more time around those younger than I. Most of my co-workers at the Health Dare were the age of my children.

I worked for Bridget for four years. Much of that time, I worked two jobs, as well as taking a one-year online course for my Health Coach certification. It was a costly certification, and Bridget paid for it., The certification meant that I had both the experience and credentials that continue to benefit me in my "career" today. In October of 2017, I left the retirement village and worked solely for Bridget until June 1, 2019.

I cannot begin to describe what a blessing Bridget was and how many times she brought joy to my life. The staff took an all-expenses-paid trip to Disney World right after I was hired. In two days, Bridget, a few friends, and co-workers, and I visited all three Disney parks twice. I was by far the oldest in the crowd and amazed that I kept up with them. I stayed in a Disney Resort and made memories that I would not otherwise have been able to make.

God uses the unexpected to help us in our times of need and in our darkest hours. In my new job, I learned to laugh again, and life became a bit lighter. Bridget looks to me more like a supermodel than a saint, but she is a saint to me. Bridget taught me true religion and reminded me again of James 1:27,

*"Pure religion and undefiled before God and the Father is this, To visit the fatherless and widows in their affliction..."*

Bridget is the one person who stands out as making a "God" difference in my journey. She is also the one person whose life in ministry convicts me the most.

In January of 2018, Bridget remarried. I drove to Greenville, South Carolina, to attend the wedding. It was a beautiful ceremony, and Josh made vows, not only to Bridget, but also to her two daughters.

On my daily prayer list, I ask God to bless Bridget, Josh, their daughters, their church, and their business, because of Bridget's kindness to me. It is my wish to pay it back and even more so, to pay it forward.

Through the past seven years, God has sent unlikely people to help me. When I say "unlikely," I mean people other than those I expected God to send but did not. I am not trying to point a finger at anyone. I have been convicted by my own lack of pure religion. I believe with all my heart that God sent the exact people I needed at just the right time.

## Starbucks Cards

In I Kings 17:10-16, we read about a widow who used the last of her oil to make a cake for the prophet Elijah. Because of her good deed, the Bible says that she borrowed every pot from every neighbor around and filled each one with oil without running out.

My "oil" in this time of trial has been Starbucks cards. My friend Jane has sent me a Starbucks card every month for seven years. That is a long time to remember someone in their grief, and that is a lot of coffee—but not too much for me.

My friend Linda has sent me a 100 dollar bill every month for almost as long. Linda is a victim of Parkinson's Disease and has fought it for decades. Still, she keeps her sweet spirit and wears the smile of a true victor. God has greatly used her in my life for encouragement. A card and an "I love you," have come every month with her cash gift.

## Tree Frogs

I have a friend, Janet, whom I have called my "tree frog." There is an Australian tree frog called the White's Tree Frog that excretes a liquid from its toe pads that causes it to be unusually good at sticking to surfaces. Some tropical tree frogs are almost impossible to remove once they are stuck to an individual.

Janet has been the one person who I have been able to count on as an active listener for several years and from the very beginning of my life change. Her friendship and her listening ear prevented me from venting to my children or anyone else. Humanly speaking, I don't know that I would have survived some of the loneliest days and months had God not sent a Janet in my life. Janet also loves to talk about Jesus—Our "God talks" have been great medicine and brought a merry heart to an otherwise inconsolable one. If you know someone who is hurting and feel God would have you to do so, just be there and listen. And lift their eyes to the only One Who can be their comfort.

To Bridget, Jane, Linda, and Janet, you have taught me what Christianity in action looks like. I will be forever grateful. I have "friended" you for life, and my unfriend button has been permanently deactivated. You are the heroines both in my hall of friendship and in my hall of faith.

## Strangers And Angels

I took my first road trip as a woman alone on Christmas Day–the first Christmas after my former husband left. The children came to my house, and we spent Christmas the way we always had. We have not done that since, and we have all since admitted that it was a terrible idea. We opened gifts, and everyone left about noon. The kids couldn't get out of the house fast enough and, honestly, I was glad to see them go. The house was too sad for anyone to stick around.

After the kids left, I packed up and drove to Michigan. It was a terribly lonely trip, driving by myself on Christmas. Halfway there, I stopped at a Burger King and had a "God moment."

I walked into the fast-food restaurant, and a young college man said, "Hi! How are you today? I really like your sweater."

The young girl beside him added, "It is beautiful."

A middle-aged lady joined them, and they all chatted with me as if they had known me all of my life. I don't know about you, but people working at the average fast-food restaurant generally don't become your best friends in five minutes or less. But they did that day. As the saying goes, "You had to be there." But it remains one of my sweetest memories from recent years. God may have replaced the regular workers with three angels, but I have never been treated like that at a restaurant before or since. I can't describe how it lifted my spirits.

I behave differently toward strangers since that day. I smile at almost everyone I meet. In the early years of being alone, I would sometimes drive to Starbucks and stay awhile just to feel human and to feel like I was a part of the human race. I was that lonely and disoriented. A kind smile from a stranger literally "snapped" me out of it, time after time. And in those dark days, a rude stranger could feel like the straw that was going to break my weary back.

We cannot know if that person we glared at for cutting us off in traffic is experiencing the worst day of their life. Maybe they didn't see us because they literally are barely making it through the day. The cashier we ignored because we were in a hurry may be supporting herself and her children for the first time in her single life.

I believe that God can use the smile of a stranger to change a life, especially if we are doing it with Jesus and for Jesus. Maybe you are at a stage of life where you feel useless when you were once useful. I have been there. Just a smile at a stranger and an, "I praise you, Jesus," speak volumes in Heaven and may be more useful than all of the autographs I signed and all of the pictures I had taken at all of the church functions put together when I was a pastor's wife.

We experience pure religion when we meet someone in their deepest need in whatever way we can. Maybe the only resource you have at your disposal is a smile–then share it. Jesus had little good to say about religion in the Bible. One time, He described it as pure, and when he did, he ascribed it to helping the helpless and the hurting. I am pointing the finger at myself when I say that my religion definitely needed to be purified. Jesus has purified my religion through examples of strangers and friends who came to me in my time of need.

## A Friend That Sticketh Closer Than A Brother

As time has passed, there have been moments when I couldn't share with my children or with my tree frog friends what God was doing in my heart. Part of this journey, I have had to walk alone. During those parts of the journey, I have been reminded of Proverbs 18:24,

> *"A man that hath friends must show himself friendly; and there is a friend that sticketh closer than a brother."*

Jesus is the ultimate tree frog. He sticks to us like glue. The Bible tells us in Psalms 139:3 that God encompasses us. Psalms 139:5 says that He is walking right behind us, standing right before us, and has His hand upon us. Psalms 33:18 says that *"the eye of the Lord is upon them that fear him."*

God stares at us. He gets in our face, and He invades our personal zone. I wonder if the angels in Heaven are ever amused as they hear us cry out, "God, where are you?" All the while, we are surrounded by a God Who is in our personal space, staring intently at us with His hand on our shoulder. I can only imagine the love in His eyes.

I have learned much about religion and friendship during the past seven years–mostly that I have a lot left to learn. I have had some awesome teachers amongst friends and even strangers.

My greatest Teacher has been my Friend Jesus. He makes an awesome Friend in the light and in the dark.

*Pure Religion*

# GLOSSARY OF SCRIPTURE

*Leviticus 19;34, "But the **stranger** that dwelleth with you shall be unto you as one born among you, and thou shalt love him as thyself; for ye were **strangers** in the land of Egypt: I am the Lord your God."*

*Deuteronomy 10:19, "Love ye, therefore, the **stranger**: for ye were **strangers** in the land of Egypt."*

*Matthew 19:19, "Honour thy father and thy mother: and, **Thou shalt love thy neighbor as thyself.**"*

*Matthew 22:39, "And the second is like unto it, **Thou shalt love thy neighbor as thyself.**"*

*Mark 12:31, "And the second is like, namely this, **Thou shalt love thy neighbor as thyself.** There is none other commandment greater than these."*

*Luke 10:27, "And he answering, said, **Thou shalt love the Lord thy God** with all thy heart, and with all thy soul, and with all thy strength, and with all thy mind, **and thy neighbor as thyself.**"*

*Romans 13:10, "Love worth no ill to his neighbor: therefore, **love is the fulfilling of the law.**"*

*Romans 15:2, "**Let every one of us please his neighbor** for his good to edification."*

*Galatians 5:14, "For all the law is fulfilled in one word, even in this; **Thou shalt love thy neighbor as thyself.**"*

*James 2:8, "If ye fulfill the royal law according to the scripture **Thou shalt love thy neighbor** as **thyself,** ye do well."*

# *Chapter 10.*
## One Thing is Needful

*O*ne of the highlights of the year 2016 was the time I spent with my mother, Beverly Hyles, during Thanksgiving. I flew to Dallas and celebrated the holiday with Mom, two of my siblings, and some of their family. I always enjoyed spending time at Mom's condo. It was such a restful time. The only thing I dreaded was the weight I always gained from her magnificent cooking.

Mom made at least one enormous dinner each time I visited. Every morning she made a large, hot breakfast, and we would sit in the kitchen at her tiny bistro table and chat.

Mom was a member of the First Baptist Church of Dallas, Texas, during the last thirteen years of her life. She taught a ladies' Sunday school class there. I always looked forward to visiting her church with her. That November 2017, as I sat in her class and watched her teach, I thought to myself, "My mom is eighty-seven, and she is beautiful." She stood before her class in a suit, with a trim figure, in heels, wearing what I call "chunky" jewelry. She was beautiful inside and out as she stood before her ladies and taught. A day or so later, I said goodbye to my mom for what would be the last time I would see her on this earth, and I flew back to North Carolina.

In May 2017, my sister Becky called me and asked if I would consider moving to Dallas. She said that Mom was beginning to seem feeble to her. Becky has had the chronic disease of Lupus for decades. Though she and her husband Tim had taken great care of Mom, there was no way that they could be her permanent caregivers.

I spoke with Mom later the same day and told her I would be glad to move to Dallas if she needed me. Her reply was, "Absolutely not!" Mom was a very independent person, and I don't think she ever wanted to live long enough to have someone take care of her. She still lived alone and drove, and she was still teaching Sunday school.

I ended the conversation by reassuring my mother that she never needed to be afraid that she would not have someone to take care of her and that whenever she needed me, I would be there. For the time being, however, we both believed that my place was still in NC.

I had grown especially close to my mom during my first years on my own. I had been a Daddy's girl and thus not nearly as close to Mom as I was to Dad. I had never known my mom apart from her very public life. It seemed that her public image overshadowed our private relationship. After 2012, however, I was able to be an ordinary daughter with an ordinary mom, entirely outside of the spotlight. I cherished that time.

## The Loss Of A Mother

I was still working as a Health Coach and part-time at the retirement village. One of my jobs as a health coach was to make "house calls" from time to time to check our clients. One evening, I drove over to a client's house. On my way home, I received a call from my niece Trina. It was August 30, 2017. She informed me that my mom had been found dead in her condo that evening. I was shocked. Mom had been such a strong woman, and though I knew she didn't ever want to live to be really old (She had told me that when I was just a young girl.) I thought she would live forever. My two grandmothers had lived to be ninety-five and ninety-seven, and my father's only sister lived to be ninety-nine. Though Becky had been worried about her, my mom had looked to me as "young" and strong as ever.

Becky had recently fallen and broken her hip. My mom had made a big pot of hamburger stew and her famous chocolate cake and taken it over to her. It was almost comical to think of my mom at the age of 88, taking care of my temporarily bedridden sister.

The last deed that we know Mom performed was to make that stew and cake. She would have loved for that to have been her final deed–my mom was an amazing cook.

I called my children and told them the news, and we all prepared to fly to Texas for her funeral. I lay awake almost all night long, alone in my townhouse, and cried for my mother.

When a child is hurting, no matter what her age, she needs her mother. I had been no exception. Mom and I had established the habit of a weekly call that usually lasted sixty to ninety minutes. I was still terribly lonely, and I am sure I wore my mom out, talking to her about all that was going on in my life and in my heart. We spent a lot of time philosophizing about life and became closer than ever before. We were two former pastor's wives, living alone and entirely taken out of the spotlight for different reasons. We found great consolation in each other. As I lay crying through the night in bed on August 30, 2017, I honestly didn't know how I was going to go on without her. There had been just so much loss.

## Mom's Bible

I flew to Dallas, and all four of my children met me there. We attended the funeral and had some time of reunion with the family. The siblings and I went to Mom's condo and went through her stuff. We really didn't take much, but we all chose one of her Bibles. Becky, as the oldest, and in many ways, the closest to my mother chose a Bible first. Then it was my turn. I intended to look at several Bibles before I chose one, but inside the first Bible I saw, on the first page was a name. The name was "Cindy." Written beside that name was the reference to a verse:

Zechariah 2:5, *"For I, saith the Lord, will be unto her a wall of fire round about, and will be the glory in the midst of her."*

"I want this Bible," I proclaimed.

I knew exactly why my mom had written my name beside that reference and approximately when. I am sure my mother was praying for me during all that happened. I sleep with my mother's Bible every night, and I cherish it.

After the funeral in Dallas, there was a memorial service in Crown Point, Indiana, where my mother is buried beside my father and grandparents. I spoke at that service. I was not excited to speak in public, but I felt I could not be a part of the service without speaking of her. I basically shared two things.

1. A thought from my devotions
2. My last conversation with my mother

## Never Taken Away

The day after my mom's death, during my daily devotions, I read Luke 10:38-42. The last verse, Luke 10:42, reminded me so much of my mother's later life.

*"But one thing is needful: and Mary hath chosen that good part, which shall not be taken away from her."*

Mary was sitting at Jesus' feet listening to Him as he visited at her house, while her sister Martha was grumbling and full of anxiety because she had no one to help her serve the food. Jesus bragged on Mary for choosing the one thing that was needful.

Beverly Hyles was one of the most talented and beautiful women I have known. She was a singer, a painter, a public speaker, an author, a teacher, and a domestic goddess, not to mention the pastor's wife of a megachurch. I never could quite fill her shoes. At eighty-eight, when Mom died, most of those opportunities had been stripped away from her because that is what life and aging do to most people.

I had also had many opportunities stripped away from me for different reasons. So, there we were, two women living alone, having experienced loss, and enjoying not just a mother/daughter relationship, but a great friendship. I so appreciated that time of life that we shared together.

I always knew that my mother walked with God, and I always knew that she prayed for me. In those last years that mom lived alone, I saw quiet contentment in her walk with God. Mom had never wanted the spotlight, and she so enjoyed her anonymity. Making hamburger stew and chocolate cake and taking it to her daughter were more her things. So was teaching a small ladies' Sunday school class and just being a faithful church member. Mom finally resigned from her Sunday school class—one week before she died.

Mostly, Mom's "thing" was reading her Bible and praying. We both had lost so much, and yet we both had a shared love for our Lord. We had what was needful, and it was never taken away from us. It couldn't be taken away from us.

## An Unsuspected Goodbye

I had no way of knowing that Sunday night before Mom's death that she would be seeing Jesus in a couple of days. I didn't know we were having our last conversation on this earth. But God made sure that we had a sweet goodbye. We had been talking for some time when Mom said something like this.

"You know Cindy, it is absolutely amazing all that you have been through. You have been strong through it all. I am really proud of you."

"Yes, Mom," I replied, "God has been very good to me."

"He has been very good to you, Cindy," she added with emphasis, "He has been very good to both of us."

And then she added, "Have a good evening, Cindy, I love you."

"Good night, Mom, I love you too!"

And that good night was goodbye on this earth.

I am so thankful that God gave me such a sweet goodbye from my mother. I am glad that we parted talking about our Friend Jesus. We had both lost so much by that time of our lives. But we both had that one thing that was needful. Mom would leave soon to see the God she loved. And I was able to reassure her that I would be left in good hands with the only One that was needful.

I did lie awake and cry most of the night on August 30, 2017. The covers were a mess when I got out of bed the following morning. I had literally writhed in soul pain. "Jesus," I cried, "I don't think that I can do without my mom. I want my mom."

"Jesus, there has just been so much loss–so. much. loss."

"Everybody goes away," was my cry in the night.

Three years later, I still miss her terribly. When a girl is hurting, she wants her mother.

When I was only five years old, she led me to the "one thing that is needful" by leading me to pray and accept Christ.

I still miss her, but I am being strong, because on the night of August 30 and every night since then, I have looked in the dark and have seen Him standing there–the One thing that is needful is a Who. And His name is Jesus.

*One Thing Is Needful*

# GLOSSARY OF SCRIPTURE

*Luke 10:38-42, "Now it came to pass, as they went, that he entered into a certain village: and a certain woman named Martha received him into her house. And she had a sister called Mary, which also sat at Jesus' feet, and heard his word. But Martha was cumbered about much serving, and came unto him, and said, Lord, dost thou not care that my sister hath left me to serve alone? Bid her therefore that she help me. And Jesus answered and said unto her, Martha, Martha, thou art careful and troubled about many things:* **But one thing is needful:** *and Mary hath chosen that good part, which shall not be taken away from her."*

# Chapter 11
## The Good Little Sunday School Girl

*I*n the book of Job, we read the story of a man who "feared God and eschewed evil." Satan wanted to prove a point to God, so he asked permission to afflict Job. God allowed Satan to do so, and Satan wreaked havoc on Job's life. Job's loss is the example of the greatest one imaginable.

My life has been compared to Job's more than once in the past seven years. I must say that I am no Job. I am not that brave or that good. But there are two ways that Job reminds me of myself. Before God allowed Job's trial to end, He showed both His greatness and Job's sinfulness. Job's pride had to be removed before his trial could be over.

I am like Job in that I have been privileged to learn more about the greatness of God in the past seven years. I have also learned more about my own sinfulness.

The year 2018 was a year in which God revealed the latter to me like never before. Many good things happened during the year, and I don't fault any other human being for what I learned about myself. But twice during that year, something came between Jesus and me.

I have always felt remarkably close to Jesus and had not been accustomed to feeling the way I did. Through it all, I have been able to distinguish more clearly what it means to fear God.

## The Fear Of God

For much of my life, though I loved Jesus, I was also afraid of Him. That is not the correct attitude that anyone should have, but that is how I often felt.

I John 4:18, "*There is no fear in love, but perfect love casteth out fear: because fear hath torment. He that feareth is not made perfect in love.*"

Fully understanding the love God has for us is the key to overcoming being afraid of Him,

And yet the Bible clearly states that "...*the fear of the Lord is the beginning of knowledge...*" Proverbs 1:7

and "...*of wisdom.*" Proverbs 9:10 and Psalms 111:10.

One of the meanings of the word "fear "in the Bible is awe or respect. When one worships God, he is demonstrating his fear of God.

But I believe I learned a new meaning of the fear of God in 2018.

In 2018, there was something I needed to let go of–something that I know was between God and me. I never felt that God was angry at me. I felt loved by Jesus every second of that year. But I slowly became aware that the proverbial "elephant in the room" was impairing my relationship with Jesus.

I was content with the way my life was going, and I didn't have a desire to make any changes. I had to make a choice: Do I make the necessary changes and risk losing some security? Or do I lose the special nothing-between relationship that I had shared with Jesus for as long as I could remember?

Humanly speaking, security has been pretty hard to come by in the last seven years. Losing security was something I feared. But my greatest fear was not to feel the favor of God upon my life. I don't believe that God's favor is something we have to earn on a day to day basis, thankfully. Otherwise, none of us would experience it. No one deserves the favor of God.

But there is much to be lost when we know God has asked us to let go of something, and we have said "no" or "not yet." These things are not always bad. Sometimes they are just things that are bad for us. This was the spiritual place that I found myself in 2018 and into 2019.

I was still attending Colonial every Sunday morning, and God was blessing me there in many sweet ways. I began visiting another church on Sunday evenings–the Beacon Baptist Church of Raleigh, NC, where I was now living. I sat between two preachers' wives while I was attending there.

One was a retired pastor's wife, Renee, who was then, and still is, nursing her retired pastor-husband through dementia. Renee was somewhat aware of the decision I was making. Renee didn't tell me what to do exactly, but she listened and advised week after week, and she showed me the love of Christ.

Renee had been a close friend of my mom's. Throughout my entire faith journey, I have been amazed by how God sends people when you need them. He sent the folks at the retirement village when I needed someone to nurture. He sent Bridget and my younger co-workers when I was missing my children, and He sent Renee when I was missing my mother.

Most Sunday evenings, I sat between Renee and Joann. Joann had been a widow for over a decade and then remarried the former pastor of Beacon. She was both feisty and loving. Joann and her husband Randy are in their eighties, and both still have beautiful singing voices. I never told them, but I looked forward each week to hearing their rich, harmonious voices singing the old hymns. I somehow felt each week that I was in the designated seat God had planned for me. Both ladies made a difference and probably never realized how much.

I slipped into Beacon very quietly every Sunday evening and slipped out, and I rarely spoke to anyone. I would describe myself as pretty unfriendly during that season. No one knew exactly what was taking place in my heart.

One Sunday evening, a guest speaker came and preached on the story in Luke 21:1-4,

> *"And he looked up and saw the rich men casting their gifts into the treasury. And he saw also a certain poor widow casting in thither two mites. And he said, Of a truth, I say unto you, that this poor widow hath cast in more than they all: For all these have of their abundance cast in unto the offerings of God: but she of her penury hath cast in all the living that she had."*

I cannot quote this man, nor do his sermon justice, but as I recall, he taught that the two mites weren't really the issue in the story. The real issue is that the poor widow was willing to give up her security for Jesus.

I never shook the guest preacher's hand. I didn't speak or acknowledge his presence. For all he knew, I could have cared less about what he had to say. I just stayed in my seat and chatted a bit with Renee. Then I drove home, got on my knees in my townhouse bedroom, and with the fear of God in my soul, I let go.

## Unknown Blessings

Heaven will be full of many wonders, not the least of which, the wonder of being able to see what God was doing in our lives, especially when we were feeling useless.

Renee, who sat on my left at Beacon, will see more clearly what God can do with a retired pastor's wife whose chief job title is "dementia caregiver."

Randy and Joann, on my right side, will understand better what God can do with a voice that doesn't resonate from the choir or the pulpit any longer, but to one searching heart. Joann will know that though she wasn't the first wife of Pastor Randy, she was the one who had the blended voice and life that I needed to see and hear.

Mike is the name of the guest speaker God used that night, and he is also a retired pastor. It is interesting how God used all of these "former ministry leaders" to influence me at that time. God used these saints to help me to choose "the fear of the Lord."

In fear of the Lord, I chose to let go, and there was nothing between my soul and the Savior any longer.

In my devotions, shortly after, I read Proverbs 21:31, "*The horse is prepared against the day of battle: but safety* (security) *is of the Lord.*"

## Dying To Self

I wish I could say that was the last time in those twelve months that I found myself with something between the Lord and me, but it wasn't. One other time, God convicted my heart that I was going about something in a way that was not completely honest. I had always valued my integrity and lived honestly before the Lord. I made a decision that was not uncommon for someone to make in a business dealing, but God pricked my heart and said my words and actions were not right. I didn't see any way out of the business venture, and I wanted to proceed very badly–so I did.

Not only am I unaccustomed to having something between God and me, but I am a horrible liar, for which I am thankful. One lie led to another, and it became pretty apparent that I needed to back out of the venture. I wasn't fooling anybody–especially God.

Honesty is something I have always taken for granted. After all, I am a good little Sunday school girl and an honest person. I was proud of my impeccable integrity. It wasn't fair that others' actions in previous years had put a blemish on my record, but at the end of the day, that was not on me.

In the year 2018, not once but twice, I saw myself for who I am and what I am capable of doing. I am a sinner–not a sort of a sinner. I am as sinful as the entire human race, and Jesus needed to die on the cross for someone just like me.

Every morning since 2018, I ask God to help me to be honest for the rest of my life and especially for the next twenty-four hours. I cannot live honestly without Him. I live honestly **because** of Him.

Don't misunderstand. I am not down on myself. I am fully aware that Jesus has me all dressed up in His righteousness.

Isaiah 61:10, "*I will greatly rejoice in the Lord, my soul shall be joyful in my God; for he hath clothed me with the garments of salvation, he hath covered me with the robe of*

*righteousness, as a bridegroom decketh himself with orna-
ments, and as a bride adorneth herself with her jewels."*

At the end of the day, all of my righteousness is Jesus' righteousness.
I am just a sinner—a sinner who has a great Savior—that is all.

I am not sure I can fully explain the atmosphere of my life during
the rest of 2018 and into the year 2019. It just seemed like everywhere
I went, and in everything I did, life kept saying to me, "You are not
important."

I was stinging from the mistakes of the past year, and I was seeing
myself in a new light—a not so pretty light.

Several times I told God, "It just seems that everything is telling me
that I am not important."

This is not a reflection of how anyone was treating me. I can't exactly
put my finger on it. But there was a long season of plodding to and from
work and feeling more alone than I had felt before.

Six years of heartache had passed. I had made several steps forward
and slipped several steps back. Looking back, God was doing some of
His greatest work in my life, and Jesus did not fail me—not. one. time.

In the early months of 2019, I finally stepped inside my cocoon and
laid down with all of my losses, failures, and yes, sins. It took almost
seven years, but in 2019, I believe that the good little Sunday school
girl was finally put to rest.

# GLOSSARY OF SCRIPTURE

*Proverbs 14:26,27, "In the **fear of the Lord** is strong confidence: and his children shall have a place of refuge. The **fear of the Lord** is a fountain of life, to depart from the snares of death."*

*Psalms 33:8, "Let all the earth **fear the Lord**: let all the inhabitants of the world stand in awe of him."*

*Psalms 33:18, "Behold, the eye of the Lord is upon them that **fear** him, upon them that hope in his mercy."*

*Proverbs 15:16, "Better is little with **the fear of the Lord** than great treasure and trouble therewith."*

*Proverbs 19:23, "The **fear of the Lord** tendeth to life: and he that hath it shall abide satisfied; he shall not be visited with evil."*

*Proverbs 23:17, "Let not thine heart envy sinners, but be thou in **the fear of the Lord** all the day long."*

*Jeremiah 32:39,40, "And I will give them one heart, and one way, that they may **fear** me for ever, for the good of them, and of their children after them. And I will make an everlasting covenant with then, that I will not turn away from them, to do them good; but I will put my **fear** in their hearts, that they shall not depart from me."*

*John 12:24, "Verily, verily, I say unto you, Except a corn of wheat fall into the ground and die, it abideth alone: but if it Die, it bringeth forth much fruit."*

*Matthew 10:39, "He that findeth his life shall lose it: and he that loseth his life for my sake shall find it."*

*Galatians 2:21, "I am crucified with Christ; nevertheless, I live; yet not I, but Christ liveth in me: and the life which I now live in the flesh I live by the faith of the Son of God, who loved me and gave himself for me."*

# Chapter 12
Starting Over Again

*I* spent Christmas 2018 in Ohio with all my children and grandchildren. Christmas afternoon, we all drove to Ken's church and sang together as a family. We have several musicians in our family, so we gathered on the platform and sang our hearts out to the Lord. I looked around and watched and listened as everyone sang. I stopped my own singing for a moment and guess what I did–I cried. The joy of the Lord was so strong in that room and also later at Ken's house when we did Christian karaoke. I couldn't help but notice the remarkable difference between the spirit of that day and the spirit of our first Christmas without their father six years before.

As I boarded the plane to go back to North Carolina a couple of days later, I was filled with praise for and gratitude to God. I knew that God had watched over my children where they were while I had been away. At the Cincinnati airport, under my breath, I hummed,

> "You're a good, good Father
> That's Who You are; That's Who You Are."

In January of 2019, God began to turn my heart towards Ohio. I have never felt anything quite like it. It seemed like I could actually feel my heart being moved. I loved North Carolina, and I loved the South. I had no desire to move back to the Midwest, until the early months of 2019. I took my time and prayed much about it. I was helped by the book "Discerning the Voice of God" by Priscilla Shirer, daughter of Tony Evans. In May, I flew to Ohio to look at houses, and on June 17, 2019, I left North Carolina.

June 16 was my last Sunday in NC. I didn't attend my home church, Colonial Baptist Church of Cary, because I hate goodbyes. I went to another church that I had visited only once before. The pastor was not preaching that day, and a man whom I did not know spoke. It was obvious that the Lord had prepared a message for me. I don't remember much about the message except that the speaker emphasized that sometimes God asks us to make a decision that is not our first choice; nonetheless, He is always working His plan in our lives.

I left the Summit Church–Raleigh campus–that day and had a good talk with Jesus as I drove home.

*Lord,*

*You know that it was my desire to grow old in North Carolina and at the Colonial Baptist Church of Cary. Being near my children and grandchildren again thrills me, and part of me can hardly wait to leave. But I am sad today, and though I don't understand what You are doing in my life, I honestly believe You are leading me to Ohio, and I trust You.*

That evening I picked up my son Ken at the airport. We ate dinner together and spent the last night in my NC townhouse. We packed up the U-Haul and started the drive to Ohio on Monday, June 17.

## Arriving In Ohio

My first two and a half months in Ohio, I spent living in the guest room in Ken and Candace's house. The guest room is in the finished basement, so I could hear every bouncing ball and the pitter-patter of every child's feet on the floor above. Candace often apologized for all the noise and confusion, but I loved it. I would lie in bed sometimes and just bask in the pure joy of noise. It was the first time I had not lived alone for an exceptionally long time. With two other adults, four children (One is a two-year-old) and three dogs, I was definitely not alone. Those were very healing weeks for me.

The months of July and August 2019 felt like one long vacation. My daughter Jaclynn had met me in Ohio when I arrived and had come to visit more than once. I was able to do some much needed reconnecting with all of my children and grandchildren.

In August, I found the perfect job for me. I was able to use my Health Coach certification to find a position in another company. My boss is a sweet Christian lady. Every day I spend at work, I am assured of God's watch care over me. I can't imagine a job that would be a better fit.

In September, I moved into my own home, just a five-minute drive from Ken and his family, and from their church. The adjustment of moving back to the Midwest was much bigger than I imagined. I found myself revisiting a lot of the things that had happened seven years prior and rethinking the decisions I had made. At the end of the day, God brought me to the same conclusions I had before, and I began to enjoy my time in Ohio.

I came to Ohio "for a season" to help my children heal. We had not been estranged during our years of living apart, and there was no tension between us. Still, I had not been able to be there for them, and I felt we needed each other. I had grown terribly lonely those last months in Raleigh.

## A New Chapter

A Christian counselor once told me that life is divided into chapters. I had hoped that my life would be just one long chapter. I wanted to grow old in my home area of Northwest Indiana, in the beautiful little town of St. John, and in the summer cottage style home that I had lived in for thirty years and almost all of my married life. I wanted to attend the same church. Life had its struggles, but I was content with life as it was.

I get attached easily, and I don't detach very well. When God started a new chapter in Durham, North Carolina, I believed that would be where the final chapter of my life story would end. Four years later, I moved to Raleigh, and a year and a half after that, I moved to Ohio. Life seemed like a maze or a seven-year wandering in the wilderness.

Looking back, I have come to see more clearly what God has been doing in my story. I have accepted that my story is going to include several different twists and turns.

## Offering To God

Just before I moved from NC, I read the book *Suffering is Never For Nothing* by Elisabeth Elliot. In this book, she relates how she struggled with her second husband's cancer. This is the woman whose first husband was murdered on the mission field by primitive tribesmen. She had returned to that mission field and lived among the people who had murdered her husband. She ranks as a super Christian in my mind.

That is why it was hard for me to believe that she struggled with her attitude toward God when her second husband was diagnosed with cancer. But she did–terribly. Then, one day, she knelt down and gave her suffering as an offering to God. That is what I did before I left NC.

I couldn't wait to be near my children, but I was distraught that I was going to start over again. I was very ready for this trial to be finished. I had come to NC six years previously to start a new life, and I did not feel that my new life had started yet.

I got on my knees again, and I gave all of the sufferings to God as an offering. I really didn't know God took suffering as an offering. It seems kind of like putting a dress with holes and stains in the Salvation Army kettle at Christmas. But it was what I had, and six years after the fact, it still seemed like suffering was what defined me. So, I gave it to Jesus.

The hardest thing to give Jesus was not the horrible nightmare of July 2012. The hardest things to hand over that night were the disappointment and resentment building inside. Here I was–starting all over again. The disappointment was what I had to offer. Instead of nursing my resentment, I gave my disappointment to God as an offering, and I set out to build a new life–again–in Ohio. My plan was to stay in Ohio awhile to help my children. God's plan was to use my children to help me.

*Starting Over Again*

# A Glossary Of Scripture

*Isaiah 43:19, "Behold, I will do a **new** thing; now it shall spring forth; shall ye not know it? I will even make a way in the wilderness and rivers in the desert."*

*II Corinthians 5:17, "Therefore if any man be in Christ, he is a **new** creature: old things are passed away; behold, all things are become **new**."*

*Ephesians 4:24, "And that ye put on the **new** man, which after God is created in righteousness and true holiness."*

*Colossians 3:10, "And have put on the **new** man, which is renewed in knowledge after the image of him that created him."*

*Hebrews 10:20, "By a **new** and living way, which he hath consecrated for us, through the veil, that is to say, his flesh."*

# *Chapter 13*
## No Fear in Love

*I* have always been told that I am transparent in my writing, and this book is turning out to be no exception. This next chapter is a little bit more difficult for me to write because I am about to confess yet another of my shortcomings.

In my "other life," I did a lot of public speaking, and I made it clear more than once that one of my besetting sins is fear.

Not long after I arrived in Ohio, my son and I were talking. Somewhere during our conversation, Ken said that he believed that God wanted to deliver me from my fear. I wish I could say that I took this humbly. Even though I was incredibly quiet, my spirit was a bit offended. I wanted to say, "DON'T TELL ME WHAT TO DO. I AM YOUR MOTHER!" I also thought about elaborating on how difficult each labor pain was, but I refrained.

Actually, Ken is a gentle, tender man by nature. He adores his children and his wife, who was his high school sweetheart. I have felt that others have used my fear against me from time to time in my life. Therefore, it has been easy for me to take offense to any admonition about it. I have heard Ken say in his preaching that we sometimes become comfortable with our sins and lose hope of seeing any change.

The truth is my fear had grown in seven years, and I had developed a bit of PTSD–Post Traumatic Stress Disorder. That disorder was manifested in a case of claustrophobia. For a while, I would not ride on an elevator. Not long after Jack was incarcerated, I found myself stuck in a gas station bathroom. It only took a minute to unjam the door, but by the time I got it loose, I bolted out in a panic. It is unusual to see a long line at a gas station bathroom. Still, as I recall, it seemed more people were waiting in line at that bathroom than at the entrance of a ride at Disney World. I am sure I looked pretty silly running out that door.

All the changes that transpired during my move from NC to Ohio had made my fears drastically worse. I rarely spoke to anyone about them, and my secret was feeling very dark and heavy.

I stopped a lady at FaithWay Church where Ken pastors and asked her to pray for me. I casually mentioned that I was a bit nervous in all of my new surroundings. She put her hand on my shoulder and prayed with me in the church fellowship hall. I wish this weren't true, but I think I can count on one hand the number of people who have prayed with me like that during my Christian life.

Strangely, my fear died down after that simple prayer with my sweet friend.

The devil doesn't give up easily, though, and I found the fear resurfacing to the point that I was desperate. I woke up one morning extremely troubled, so troubled that I decided to fast for the day. I don't usually tell people when I fast, and my fasting is rare and wimpy. Generally, I fast for twenty-four hours, from dinner to dinner. I love to eat, and when I fast for twenty-four hours, you know that I am pretty desperate.

I recall kneeling down and praying that morning, and guess what? I was also crying. My tires needed to be replaced, and Ken was supposed to meet me at the tire shop that morning, so I could drop off my car. I prayed and asked God to show me if I should talk to Ken about my recent fears. I am cautious about what burdens I place on my children.

When I got in the car with Ken, he mentioned that he was a little late because, as he said, "I just finished talking to a pastor friend who is experiencing some spiritual warfare."

Something–or Someone–inside of me said, "That is your cue."

"Ken," I said, "I think I am struggling with some PTSD from all that has happened in these past years. I haven't really shared this with anyone, but I need to." I proceeded to tell him about my recent fear.

Sometime during that conversation, Ken took my hand and prayed with me and asked Jesus to deliver me from my fear. This was the beginning of a great spiritual victory in my life.

As of this writing, I attend church at FaithWay Church of West Chester, Ohio, where my son and his wife pastor. Many members of this church are young converts. FaithWay is a praying church.

When I was a child, prayer meetings were a dreaded experience. I mostly participated when visiting other churches. A mimeographed list was passed around with names of people who needed prayer. It was evident that the list had not been updated for several years–maybe decades. I am making fun of myself when I say I was very turned off by public prayer.

Though I treasure my time alone with the Lord, I have experienced firsthand how the devil uses isolation from God's people to snare us in his traps. I am most comfortable when I am alone with the Lord. But God has revealed to me how much I need the local church. Jesus has answered so many of my personal prayers, but I have seen Him work miracles in recent days through the prayers of His church.

Prayer and fellowship with God's people are Biblical methods for spiritual healing. I have come to value deliberate, scheduled time with fellow believers when we study God's Word and share what is on our hearts. No gossip, no slander, no shame, no judging–just a safe time to grow in the Lord.

> James 1:15, *"Confess your faults one to another, and pray one for another, that ye may be healed, The effectual fervent prayer of a righteous man availeth much."*

During this chapter of my life, I have been attending church with several new converts. We are frequently asked to find someone with whom to pray during our church services- perhaps someone we don't know well. Recently, I prayed with a new convert who shared with me that she had never prayed in front of anyone before. Our prayer time together was so sacred. I cherished hearing this sister in Christ, who was obviously talking to a new Friend. During the prayer, she mentioned to God that something "sucks." I laughed under my breath.

I am not at all surprised that this same Christian is the first person to whom I spilled the beans about writing this book. She has been a great support and prayer warrior and will have a part in however this book is used.

Sometime during the year 2019, I began to wave goodbye to my old friend, fear. I came to Ohio to help my children. Instead, they have prayed with me and helped me.

I came to FaithWay to shed some influence on these new converts. Instead, they have prayed with me and encouraged me.

Jesus came to eat with the Publicans and sinners. I was willing to do the same. Somewhere along the line, Jesus asked me to consider that maybe I was one of the Publicans and sinners. "Really, Lord?" I responded. "Why yes, I had never looked at it that way."

I came to be a help and found that I was the one in need of help. I was the one who needed prayer. And with fear in my rearview mirror—there was Someone else who was waiting to meet with me.

## GLOSSARY OF SCRIPTURE

*Matthew 17:21, "Howbeit this kind goeth not out but by **prayer** and **fasting**."*

*Matthew 21:22, "And all things, whatsoever ye shall ask in **prayer**, believing, ye shall receive."*

*Mark 9:29, "And he said unto them, This kind can come forth by nothing, but by **prayer** and **fasting**."*

*Mark 11:24, "Therefore I say unto you, What things soever ye desire, when ye **pray** believe that ye receive them, and ye shall have them."*

*Luke 1:37, "For with God nothing shall be impossible."*

*James 5:13-15, "Is any among you afflicted: let him **pray**. Is any merry: let him sing psalms. Is any sick among you? Let him call for the elders of the church; and **let them pray over him, anointing him with oil in the name of the Lord**."*

*Matthew 9:10,11,12, "And it came to pass, as Jesus sat at meat in the house, behold, many publicans and sinners came and sat down with him and his disciples. And when the Pharisees saw it, they said unto his disciples, Why eateth your master with publicans and sinners? But when Jesus heard that, he said unto them, They that be whole need not a physician, but they that are sick. But go ye and learn what that meant, I will have mercy and not sacrifice, for I came not to call the righteous, but sinners to repentance."*

# *Chapter 14*
## The Holy Spirit

*M*y father emphasized the Holy Spirit a lot in his ministry, and I recall him receiving a great deal of flack about it. I also remember some amazing miracles taking place during some of the invitations throughout those years. There were no healing lines or talking in tongues in the services, but some miraculous events did occur.

Dad's preaching series on the Holy Spirit was one of my favorites. I began as a young woman to emphasize the Holy Spirit in my own life. Somewhere along the line, that simply stopped.

I felt close to Jesus, and I asked Jesus to fill me with His Spirit daily, but the focus was markedly different, and I never noticed. I moved to Ohio in the middle of my son's preaching series on "Receiving the Holy Spirit." I saw a joyful spirit in both my son and daughter-in-law that I had not noticed in the past.

I had peace in my life, but I still felt like I was wandering through the wilderness of fear and brokenness. I was making it through each day by focusing on Jesus' love for me, but I just couldn't seem to walk away from the hurt that I had experienced. I suppose in some way it was still defining me. Though I still prayed in Jesus' name and to Jesus, I began to talk to the Holy Spirit in a way that I had done decades ago.

> John 16:7, "*Nevertheless I tell you the truth; It is expedient for you that I go away: for if I go not away, the Comforter will not come unto you; but if I depart, I will send him unto you.*"

To be honest, for most of my life, I have read that verse and doubted that it was really "expedient" for Jesus to go away, In the past seven years, there have been so many times when I have longed to see Jesus' face and to hear Jesus' voice. And yet I have heard His voice many, many times through the voice of His Holy Spirit.

Recently, I have been emphasizing the Holy Spirit in my life again. I have been talking to Him and asking Jesus to allow me to be baptized with the Holy Spirit. This is not a spooky experience, nor is it a work of the law that is to be added to salvation.

The Bible teaches us that the Holy Spirit is a token of God and of our inheritance in Heaven.

> II Corinthians 5:5, *Now he that hath wrought us for the selfsame thing is God, who also hath given unto us the earnest of the Spirit."*

My Defined King James Bible says the word **earnest** in this passage means **token.** Just as God has used things like butterflies, rainbows, and hummingbirds through the years as tokens of His love for me, so the Holy Spirit is the ultimate token of God's love and of what He has prepared for us in Heaven through salvation.

The filling of the Holy Spirit is a work of grace, as is salvation. You just have to ask for it.

> Luke 11:13, *"If ye then, being evil, know how to give good gifts unto your children: how much more shall your heavenly Father give the Holy Spirit to them that ask him?"*

## Don't Judge Yourself

For much of my life, I felt that salvation was free, but that I had to judge myself to see if there was anything in the way of the Holy Spirit's power on my life. And honestly–the same Cindy who cannot be good enough to earn salvation could never be good enough to earn the power and authority of God's Holy Spirit. Looking back, I realize that crippled me in my Christian life.

Now one of my favorite verses is where Paul speaks (through the Holy Spirit) in I Corinthians 4:3:

*"But with me, it is a very small thing that I should be judged of you, or of man's judgment: yea, I JUDGE NOT MINE OWN SELF."*

I don't know if I am a good Christian or not. If I think I am, that may be a good sign that I am not. I don't know if I was a good wife or if I am a good mother. During the past seven years, I have quit judging myself. Only God knows whether or not I am a good Christian.

Matthew 7:1, *"Judge not, that ye be not judged."*

When I quit judging myself, I felt free to stop judging others. I became able to love my brothers and sisters in Christ. I even was able to love those who are steeped in the immoral sins of this society. I do not love their sin—I hate it—hopefully as much as I hate my own. I pray daily that I will not grow accustomed to the sins of America and of this world. But I love the sinner because my sins look to Jesus the way their sins look to me—and probably much worse.

Salvation and the Holy Spirit are free gifts to those who ask. Several times each day, I ask the Holy Spirit to fill me with His power and help me to walk in His authority. And I talk to the Holy Spirit.

I worship my Father, God.
I worship Jesus Christ, the Son of God.
And I worship the Holy Spirit of God.

Jesus is always right, and He said it was expedient (needful, profitable, useful) for Him to go away, so the Holy Spirit could come to us. Can you imagine how it must hurt the heart of Jesus and the Father when Christians are afraid to speak of the Holy Spirit, fearing they will be criticized by their brothers and sisters in Christ?

Jesus said He was sending us a Helper and a Comforter. Would Jesus want us to ignore the Helper that He sent? Would it not hurt Jesus to hear us criticize the work of the Comforter that He provided for us?

The devil has a counterfeit for almost everything. We cannot always know where those counterfeits are. That is why we have been commanded to leave the tares with the wheat, lest we destroy the wheat along with the tares. This is why Jesus tells us to wait for Him to judge. He alone really knows the heart of man. He alone has true justice. I have been comforted many times in the past seven years in the realization that someday God will make all things just.

> I Corinthians 4:5, "**Therefore judge nothing** before the time, until the Lord come, who both will bring to light the hidden things of darkness, and will make manifest the counsel of the hearts: and then shall every man have praise of God."

## Deliverance

In 2019, I began to talk to the Holy Spirit again. I praise God, my Father, I praise Jesus Christ, the Son of God, and I praise the Holy Spirit. And I beg throughout the day for the filling of the Holy Spirit on my life.

I was taught from a child, that the Holy Spirit lives in me. I never really got excited about it until recently. Now I stand, and I walk in total awe that this amazing Power and Authority lives in me. He is a precious Help and Comfort, and He is an awesome Force and Protector.

I feel like the man in John 9 who received his sight. Jesus healed him, and the Pharisees were not happy with Jesus' methods. They were unconventional and "out of the box" to them. When they sought the man whose sight had been restored and said, "we know that this man is a sinner," the young man responded.

John 9:25, *"He answered and said, Whether he be a sinner or no, I know not: one thing I know, that, whereas I was blind, now I see."*

I don't understand God, the Father. I tried to put Him in my box, and seven years ago, I realized that He had never climbed in with me. He has spent the past seven years, showing me how big He is and how much He loves the world. I don't understand Him, but I trust Him.

I don't understand Jesus Christ, the Son of God. Why would He do what He did and live as He did–for my sins–for me? I don't understand Him, but I believe in Him.

I don't understand the Holy Spirit. I don't understand His supernatural ways. I don't know how I could feel so close to Jesus and still need the Holy Spirit so much in my life. I don't understand the Holy Spirit, but I needed Him. I needed His deliverance.

I needed a miracle. I needed Something or Someone who could do a makeover–a supernatural work of healing in my life. I needed a transformation. And if you are honest, you might need a miracle too. Our country and our world need a miracle.

## Transformation

During my first year in North Carolina, I stooped down to look at a large monarch butterfly near my townhouse. I came within inches of it, and the butterfly never flew away. It let me get awfully close–nose to nose–and stare at it. When I got so close, I saw a large tear in the butterfly's wing.

*"That is why it let me get so close. It can't fly. It has a large tear in its wing."* I thought.

Then almost immediately after I had that thought, the butterfly flew away.

About a week later, I was going to exercise at the gym, and I saw an identical large butterfly on a bush with the same tear in its wing. It seemed like a "God moment" to me.

And I said to myself, "That will be me. I will fly again someday, but with a broken wing".

I did not want to write a book again. I didn't want to "put myself out there." I wanted to be private. I really wanted to run and to keep hiding. But the Holy Spirit of God...

Where you see the Holy Spirit working, you see unity, grace, boldness, and miracles.

When I began to put the Holy Spirit back in His rightful place in my focus, I knew I had to use my spiritual gift for Jesus.

## Complete

For seven years, I have been telling Jesus how broken I am. I always felt He understood, and I believe He did. A few months ago, I repeated it, "Jesus, I feel so broken."

A voice inside me said, "Stop saying you are broken."

Yes, Holy Spirit, Yes, Jesus, Yes, my Father. "I am not broken; I am complete!"

And so now I fly–but not with a broken wing as I expected. That is not how my Jesus heals, and that is not how the power of His Spirit delivers. I fly, and I am whole again. I am complete; I am transformed.

"Jesus, please give me more of your Holy Spirit."

And He answered, "So glad you asked; I have been waiting. And now we must get busy, Cindy; we have a story to tell."

*The Holy Spirit*

# GLOSSARY OF SCRIPTURE

*John 14:16-18, "And I will pray for the Father, and he shall give you another Comforter, that he may abide with you for ever; Even the **Spirit of truth**; whom the world cannot receive, because it seeth him not, neither knoweth him: but ye know him; for he dwelleth with you, and shall be in you. I will not leave your comfortless: I will come to you."*

*John 14:26, "But the Comforter, which is the **Holy Ghost**, whom the Father will send in my name, he shall teach you all things, and bring all things to your remembrance, whatsoever I have said unto you."*

*John 15:26, "But when the Comforter is come, whom I will send unto you from the Father, even the **Spirit of truth**, which proceeded from the Father, he shall testify of me."*

*John 16:7, "Nevertheless I tell you the truth; It is expedient for you that I go away: for if I go not away, the Comforter will not come unto you; but if I depart, I will send him unto you."*

*John 16:13,14, " Howbeit when he, the **Spirit of truth**, is come, he will guide you into all truth: for he shall not speak of himself; but whatsoever he shall hear, that shall he speak: and he will shew you things to come. He shall glorify me: for he shall receive of mine and shall shew it unto you."*

*John 20:22, "And when he had said this, he breathed on them, and saith unto them, Receive ye the **Holy Ghost:**"*

*Acts 1:8, "But ye shall receive power, after that the **Holy Ghost** is come upon you: and ye shall be witnesses unto me both in Jerusalem, and in all Judaea, and in Samaria, and unto the uttermost parts of the earth."*

*Romans 8:9-11, "But ye are not in the flesh, but in the **Spirit**, if so be that the **Spirit of God** dwell in you. Now if any man have not the **Spirit of Christ**, he is none of his. And if Christ be in you, the body is dead because of sin; but the **Spirit** is life because of righteousness. But if the **Spirit** of him that raised up Jesus from the dead dwell in you, he that raised up Christ from the dead shall also quicken your mortal bodies by his **Spirit** that dwelleth in you."*

*I Corinthians 2:5, "That your faith should not stand in the wisdom of men, but in the power of God."*

*I Corinthians 2:10, "But God hath revealed them unto us by his **Spirit**: for the **Spirit** searcheth all things, yea, the deep things of God."*

*I Corinthians 6:19, "What? Know ye not that your body is the temple of the **Holy Ghost**, which is in you, which ye have of God, and ye are not your own?"*

*II Corinthians 3:17, "Now the Lord is that **Spirit**: and where the **Spirit of the Lord** is, there is liberty."*

*II Corinthians 5:5, "Now he that hath wrought us for the selfsame thing is God, who also hath given unto us the earnest of the **Spirit**."*

*Ephesians 4:3,4, "There is one body, and one **Spirit**, even as ye are called in one hope of your calling; One Lord, one faith, one baptism."*

*Matthew 13:25-30, "But while men slept, his enemy came and sowed tares among the wheat, and went his way. But when the blade was sprung up and brought forth fruit, then appeared the tares also. So, the servants of the householder came and said unto him, Sir, didst not thou sow good seed in thy field? From whence then hath it tares? He said unto them, An enemy hath done this. The servants said unto him, Wilt thou that we go and gather them up? But he said, Nay; lest while ye gather up the tares, ye root up also the wheat with them. Let both grow together until the harvest: and in the time of harvest I will say to the reapers, Gather ye together first the tares, and bind them in bundles to burn them: but gather the wheat into my barn."*

# Chapter 15
## The Year of the Song

*T*hroughout my life, even into adulthood, I have had almost a child-like innocence about my love for life. I had a beautiful perennial garden at my house in Indiana. As each type of flower bloomed in the spring and summer, I would literally get down on my knees and not only smell the flower, but I would also look as deep into the flower as possible. This is just one small example of how much I loved life and how greatly I enjoyed noticing God's creation and His love for me. In July of 2012, the childlike innocence and joy faded.

I loved to sing! One of my favorite places to sing was on the way home from church. It was a thirty-minute drive from church to my house in St. John, Indiana. I would drive along the winding roads that took me home, and I would sing at the top of my lungs.

I kept singing after I moved to North Carolina, but my songs were more like a fight song. I would literally yell the words to "10,000 Reasons" as a way of blocking out the sadness and showing God that I was not going to give up on praising Him.

"Bless the Lord, Oh my soul, Oh my soul
Worship His holy name.
I'll sing like never before, Oh my soul
I'll worship His Holy name."

The words came out more like a roar than a melody.

Throughout the years, from time to time, I would notice the song coming back, and I really tried to make it happen. I was generally able to sing and praise in church, but I didn't sing otherwise.

On January 1, 2020, I declared that this year was going to be for me, "The Year of the Song." Now I sing all the time. There is something different about my singing now. It is as natural as breathing to sing along with the Christian songs that resonate from my iphone. I am becoming one of those obnoxious people who sing or hum under my breath at the grocery store and at work. I walk through the neighborhood with my chihuahua, and I catch myself singing.

I love the story in 2 Kings 5:1-14 when Naaman, captain of the host of the king of Syria, is healed from his leprosy. I love it that a displaced servant girl, who could have been very bitter, made it into the Bible by wishing good for one of her captors. As she was doing her daily chores, she spoke some words that would be the catapult for one of the greatest illustrations of salvation in the Bible. She told her mistress (boss) that she thought Naaman should go to see the prophet Elisha to be healed of his leprosy. Naaman did go to see the prophet, and after a lot of coaxing, he obeyed Elisha's orders and dipped himself seven times in the dirty Jordan River.

2 Kings 1:14, *"Then went he down, and dipped himself seven times in Jordan, according to the saying of the man of God, and his flesh came again like unto the flesh of a little child, and he was clean."*

The Bible doesn't say that when Naaman was healed of his leprosy his flesh went back to normal. His flesh was not the flesh of a grizzled army captain. His flesh became like the flesh of a child.

I believe that is exactly the way the Holy Spirit heals. He can restore the childhood innocence and love for life that the devil so frequently steals from God's people.

John 10:10, *"The thief cometh not, but for to steal, and to kill, and to destroy; I am come that they might have life and that they might have it more abundantly."*

THE YEAR OF THE SONG

I have witnessed all that the devil can steal and destroy. I have also experienced how Jesus can heal.

There is a song that is sung by Christian artist Steve Green that I You Tube on my phone from time to time. It is entitled "Bring Back the Glory."

"All the laughter is gone,
And the sound of the song that we sang
Slowly faded away.
Simple joys that we knew
When we walked close with you hand in hand
In the cool of the day.
Are just memories,
Or are they dreams?
Yet we hold to the hope
That the music will come back again.
Bring back the Glory!
Won't you show us what life is for?
Bring back the Glory!
Make us open once more.
Bring back the music, the trust, the wonder
That's just like a child who has never known pain.
Bring back the Glory
The Glory again!"

This is and has been my hope and prayer–that God would preserve and restore the childlike joy and trust I once knew. We don't have to respond to life's hurts with a "worst-case scenario–I don't trust anybody" outlook. Jesus can restore what the devil has stolen.

Allow me to share the next verse:

"Give me a cause that is grand,
And a reason to stand
That calls for the best I can see.
Something worthy to live for,
A reason to give
Everything that I ever could be.
Oh, there must be more!
Take me, Lord,
How I need you to give me a glimpse of eternity."
The Holy Spirit of Jesus IS the Glory! And I often sing to Him this
final chorus of the beautiful song:
"You are the Glory!
You have shown me what life is for.
You are the Glory!
Make me open once more.
You are the music! The trust! The wonder that's just
Like a child who has never known pain!
You are the Glory!
That brings us together again."
And so, I trust again...


And so, I wonder like a child again at this abundant life that Jesus and
His Holy Spirit have given me.

And so, I sing again in 2020 -the year of the song!

*The Year Of The Song*

# GLOSSARY OF SCRIPTURE

*Psalms 40:3, "And he hath put a **new song** in my mouth, even praise unto our God: many shall see it, and fear, and shall trust in the Lord."*

*Zephaniah 3:17, "The Lord thy God in the midst of thee is mighty; he will save, he will rejoice over thee with joy, he will rest in his love, **he will joy over thee with singing**."*

*Psalms 69:30, "I will praise the name of God with a **song** and will magnify him with thanksgiving."*

*Psalms 96:1, "O **sing** unto the Lord a **new song**: **sing** unto the Lord, all the earth."*

*Psalms 98:1, "O **sing** unto the Lord a **new song**; for he hath done marvelous things: his right hand and his holy arm hath gotten him the victory."*

*Psalms 108:1, "O God, my heart is fixed; I will **sing** and give praise, even with my glory."*

*Psalms 118:14, "The Lord is my strength and **song**, and is become my salvation."*

*Psalms 149:1, "Praise ye the Lord. **Sing** unto the Lord a **new song**, and his praise in the congregation of saints."*

# Conclusion

II *Corinthians 5:21, "For he hath made him to be sin for us, who knew no sin; that we might be made the righteousness of God in him."*

I will end this story in the place where my healing began–in a courtroom. Over 2,000 years ago, Someone stood in a courtroom when He didn't belong there. The charges against Him were as foreign to Him as Heaven is to Hell. The defendant's name was Jesus. He was completely humiliated before an angry crowd for unspeakable deeds–and for deeds that I have done. The amazing thing is that the whole situation was never out of Jesus' control.

I stood in a courtroom seven years ago, where the situation was entirely out of my control. I still remember the exact moment that I knew our family was going to be broken, and that prison was going to be a part of our family's future. I walked around the house, looking at so many family pictures and knowing the inevitable was going to happen. It was completely out of my control.

Jesus had the authority and the power to bring His entire trial to a different conclusion. He was innocent, and He could have proven it–in less time than it takes for a heart to beat–but He didn't. He came instead to declare the innocence of an entire world that He loved. He came to declare me to be innocent. And He came to declare you to be innocent also. He loves you.

He left His home and had His entire lifestyle changed. Hebrews 7:25 says that Jesus became us.

*"**For such an high priest became us**, who is **holy, harm-less**, undefiled, separate from sinners, and made higher than the heavens."*

Jesus allowed His earthly possessions to be taken from Him, and He let His friends walk away. He accepted Capital Punishment and felt the pain of Hell.

Seven years ago, I felt the tiniest bit of what Jesus went through, but I am not the hero of this story. I am the guilty. I would have changed my plight if I could have. But I absolutely could not. Jesus absolutely could. But He didn't! Why? He loves you.

Worst of all, Jesus was forsaken by God. I was never forsaken by God. Not. One. Time. Jesus died on the cross for my sins because Jesus knew how much I would need God by my side and in my heart all the time.

Do you get that? God forsook God so that no forsaken spouse would ever be truly alone. God turned his back on His Son so that you and I would have a Father Who never leaves us. Why? Because He loves you.

God loves the person who may be reading this who isn't even ready to admit that their sin is indeed sin. And if I could get a loudspeaker that would reach all the way to wherever you are right now, this is what I would tell you. I would tell you that God loves you.

I John 4:19. *"We love him because he first loved us."*

If you could understand how much He loves you, right now, as you are, afraid to let go of your sin, and if you knew who He is, you would ask Him to be your God and your Savior–and He would–in a heartbeat. If you asked Him one time–He would stick around forever. That is just the kind of Friend He is. All you have to do is ask. Just once.

I would like to tell you that we are all sinners, but your sin is not your identity, although the world tries harder and harder to convince you that it is your identity. Your sin is what you do. You ARE loved by God. That is who you are.

I wrote this book for two reasons:

1. I wanted to do my part to bring glory to Jesus.

2. I wanted YOU to know that Jesus loves you.

This book is not about my family and me. We still have a lifetime of choices to make. I plan on continuing to hang on to Jesus. But I might let you down. We might let you down. But Jesus won't. He didn't let me down.

This book is about Jesus. This book is about how much Jesus loves me. This book is about how much Jesus loves YOU.

That book is about what I learned about Jesus in the dark–and in the light. And this is what I want YOU to know.

> John 3:16, *"For God so loved the world, that he gave his only begotten Son, that whosoever believeth in him should not perish, but have everlasting life."*

Thank you for sharing this book with me.

# References

## Music

**Whom Shall I Fear? (God of Angel Armies)** 11/9/2012, 1. Burning Lights, Six Steps Sparrow, 2013, Chris Tomlin, Contemporary Christian

**10,000 Reasons (Bless the Lord)** 7/12,2011, 4.10,000 reasons, Kingsway Music, 2011, Matt Redman, Worship, Contemporary

**Good, Good Father,** 10/2/2015, 1.Never Lose Sight, Sixsteps, 2015, Chris Tomlin, Contemporary Worship

**Bring Back the Glory**, 1996, The Early Years, Sparrow Records SPD1542, 1996, Steve Green, Christian Gospel

## Books

Elliot, Elisabeth, Suffering is Never for Nothing. B&H Publishing Group.

Lucado, Max, (2002). A Love Worth Giving: Living in the Overflow of God's Love. Thomas Nelson Publishers.

Richards, Dr. James B., (1990). The Gospel of Peace. Milestones International Publishers.

Shirer, Priscilla A., (2017). Discerning the Voice of God: How to Recognize When God Speaks. LifeWay Press.

## DVD

*Life Changing Prayer [DVD]* Jim Cymbala. USA Zondervan.

CPSIA information can be obtained
at www.ICGtesting.com
Printed in the USA
LVHW032120051220
673449LV00005B/893